THOUSAND PIECES OF GOLD

Thousand Pieces of Gold

a biographical novel
by Ruthanne Lum McCunn

Beacon Press   Boston

Beacon Press
25 Beacon Street
Boston, Massachusetts 02108

Beacon Press Books
are published under the auspices of
the Unitarian Universalist Association of Congregations.

99

Library of Congress Cataloging-in-Publication Data

McCunn, Ruthanne Lum.
  Thousand pieces of gold.

  (Asian voices) (Beacon paperbacks)
  1. Bemis, Polly, 1853–1933 — Fiction. 2. Chinese
Americans — History — Fiction.   I. Title.   II. Title:
1000 pieces of gold.   III. Series.
PS3563.C353T5 1988   813'.54   88-47881
ISBN 0-8070-8317-8 (pbk.)

To Don
for making it possible

PREFACE

THOUSAND PIECES OF GOLD tells the story
of Lalu Nathoy, later known as Polly Bemis. A few
fictitious characters have been added and certain
events transposed for the sake of the narrative, but
the essential story of Polly's life remains accurate.
This accuracy would have been impossible without
the help of a great many people to whom I am
deeply indebted.

First and foremost, I wish to acknowledge the
pioneer men and women who cared enough about
Polly to record her story in private papers, newspapers, journals, and oral histories.

I am grateful to historian Sister Mary Alfreda
Elsensohn for directing me to a number of these
sources and to persons still living who actually
knew Polly. Without her extensive knowledge and
generosity, my task would have been much more
difficult, if not impossible.

During my research in Idaho, I was fortunate to
have the cooperation of many people who agreed to
interviews, provided additional leads to other persons and source materials, and continued to answer
my questions via correspondence. I am particularly
indebted to Jim Campbell, John Carrey, Mary Long
Eisenhaver, Marybelle and Paul Filer, Denis G.

Long, Verna McGrane, June Sawyer, Vera Weaver Waite, and Inez Wildman.

I am also grateful to Nellie McClelland at the Idaho County Free Press, Bob Waite at the Idaho County Recorder's Office, and M. Gary Bettis, Jim Davis, Karin E. Ford, and Kenneth J. Swanson at the Idaho State Historical Society for uncovering critically needed information; to Bob Hawley at Ross Valley Books for introducing me to books about the real West; and to the librarians at San Francisco Public Library's Inter-library Loan Department who never failed to secure the books and papers I requested from libraries all across the United States.

To the many friends who gave their time and talents to the critical reading of my manuscript, I say thank you. I am especially grateful to Beverly Braun, Hoi Lee, Ellen Yeung, and Judy Yung whose insights and specialized knowledge contributed largely to the final form of this book; to John Carrey and Bob Hawley who read the manuscript for historical accuracy; and to Lynda D. Preston whose editorial skills gave my prose needed polish.

Finally, it must be said that without my husband's contributions at every stage in the research and writing of this book, *THOUSAND PIECES OF GOLD* would still only be a dream.

To him, and to Lalu Nathoy who inspired this effort, I owe my largest debt.

Ruthanne Lum McCunn

There is no history,
only fictions of varying degrees of plausibility.
Voltaire

PART ONE

第一部份

1865-1872

ONE

Outwardly they acted the same as any other evening. In the courtyard, between the outhouse and manure pit, Lalu crouched over the wooden tub, washing the pots and bowls from supper. At the opposite corner, near the door to the kitchen, her father, with his queue neatly coiled above his sun-bronzed face, leaned against the crumbling brick wall smoking his pipe. Seated on a stool beside him, her mother nursed the baby while A Cai, her younger brother, showed off, scratching out new characters in the hard dirt beneath her feet. But Lalu, scrubbing and rinsing as quickly as her fingers allowed, knew nothing was the same.

There was the unusual number of bowls and pots to wash, the delicious dinner she could still taste in the linings of her mouth, the sure knowledge that her stomach would know no hunger in the coming year, the hushed expectancy they shared. For the harvest had been exceptional. The best in all Lalu's thirteen years.

Inside the house, the platform suspended above the brick bed curved from the weight of stored sweet potatoes. The huge earthen jars in the kitchen brimmed with salted vegetables. All the baskets overflowed with dried string beans and turnip and sweet potato slices. Bundles of peanut and sweet potato vines and stalks of millet covered half the kitchen in piles higher than Lalu could reach. And, best of all, in the hiding place behind the stove...

Lalu leaped to her feet, frightening the chickens that pecked and scratched in the dirt around her, setting them to a loud squawking. For a moment she tottered on her little four-inch bound feet. Then, regaining her balance, she returned the bowls and pots to their proper shelf in the kitchen, emptied the tub of dirty dish water into the open drain behind the outhouse, and perched herself on the stool across from her father.

"Baba, the autumn breeze is chilly. It must be getting late," she prompted.

Her mother smiled and her father's eyes twinkled as he inhaled deeply, then forced the smoke out of his ears in little puffs.

Laughing, but refusing to be sidetracked, Lalu continued, "Look, the first star is out, and I hear mosquitoes."

She signaled A Cai who, arms whirring, began prancing around them in wild circles. Bewildered by the sudden noise and activity, A Fa stopped nursing and looked around. Lalu scooped him up and circled her father, humming and swinging the child until the baby's puzzled frown became delighted laughter.

Chuckling, her father put down his pipe. "Enough! Enough!" he said, swatting A Cai playfully. We'll go in."

Lalu, tossing the baby triumphantly, followed her father, mother, and brother into the kitchen.

"Let me dig it up!" A Cai demanded.

His mother handed him the metal scoop. "Be careful," she said. "Don't break the pot."

Lalu jiggled the baby. She rested all her weight on one foot, then the other. "What if someone stole it while we were at the threshing grounds?"

Her mother clapped a hand over Lalu's mouth. "Don't even say such a thing."

"Then where is it?" Lalu mumbled through her mother's fingers.

Her father peered over A Cai's shoulder. "A little to the left," he said. "Good. Now up a bit."

"I feel it," A Cai shouted.

He bobbed up, face flushed and streaked with soot, triumphantly cradling the pot of hoarded coins.

"Let me count it," Lalu asked.

"No, me. I go to school, you don't," A Cai said. "I'm older."

"Shh," their mother said. "No squabbling or tears to bring bad luck." She took the pot from A Cai. "If you want the family to have a big ox, a strong mule, two donkeys, three or four good houses, and many large and good pieces of land, you must learn to work hard like your father. It was his skill and labor that earned these coins. He will count them."

Her face glowing with excitement and pride, she handed the pot to her husband. His large brown hands which fit so comfortably around a plow fumbled with the coins as, one by one, he counted them into little piles of ten. A Fa reached out and toppled the piles.

"No, no," their mother said, taking him from Lalu. "This money is not to play with. We will use it to buy two more mu of land."

"And a cow too so I can go to the meadow with the other boys?" A Cai asked.

"Yes, and a cow too," their mother laughed. "But not so you can go to the meadow. A farmer with twelve mu of land should not have to borrow a cow for plowing."

"Is it true, Baba?" Lalu asked. "Do we really have enough for a cow as well as land?"

Her father, his eyes fever bright, scooped up the coins and held them in his upturned palms, like a person testing their weight.

"We will buy no land and no cow," he said. "Not yet. With this money, I'll lease all the land I can get and plant winter wheat. The money from that will make us rich."

ONE

Lalu gasped. Only the big land owners, the ones who could afford risks, planted winter wheat.

Her mother's arms tightened around A Fa until he began to cry. "No," she breathed. "You can't mean it."

"Why not?"

"Because it's crazy. We have pinched and hoarded for four years to get this money, and now you want to gamble it away."

Lalu wrapped her arms around A Cai who had begun to whimper. Together they backed away as their father shouted above the baby's plaintive wail.

"Four years of hard work and doing without to save enough for two mu of land and one small cow. And six years before that for just one mu. And two before that for a donkey! Winter wheat is the best crop there is. One good harvest and we can buy five, maybe six mu. And an ox besides."

"What if the harvest is bad?"

"It won't be. I feel lucky."

"That's what the gamblers in the taverns say while their wives and children beg in tatters on the street." She pulled A Cai from Lalu and thrust him and the wailing baby up before their father. "Think of your sons. What will you leave them?"

"The farm is my concern, not yours. I will hear no more about it."

At home no one dared speak of what her father and Chen, his newly hired laborer, did each day in the fields. But it seemed to Lalu that in the shops, down by the levee walls, at the wells, and in the fields, the villagers spoke of little else.

There was no escaping their talk. Even here, on the river bank where she had come to wash the baby's soiled diapers, she could hear the men's voices drifting from the square where they gathered to smoke, knit straw raincoats, weave baskets, and mend tools.

"Have you heard about Nathoy?"

"You mean that fool that leased all that land for winter wheat?"

"Used up all his savings and mortgaged his own farm besides."

Lalu pounded the rags against the rocks, wishing the slap of wet fabric would drown out their voices.

"What kind of a turtle's egg would stake his farm on such a gamble?"

"Who can say? Maybe he's got the right idea. Already his fields are green with newly sprouted seedlings."

"Yes, and yesterday's rain was perfect. Not heavy, but generous. Just the kind seedlings need to grow strong before the first snow."

"But what if there isn't another rain like the one yesterday? If it stays dry and the seedlings don't grow enough before the first snow?"

"Or if they do grow and the snow doesn't come?"

"Or if there isn't enough snow to cover the wheat and keep it safe until spring?"

"Or if it rains instead? Cold, sleety rain, the kind that kills unprotected seedlings."

The possibilities, one worse than the other, hurtled down on Lalu, pushing her back on her haunches, and all at once she felt paralyzed by the same fear that had gripped her when her father had told the story of Guo Ju, the filial son.

"Guo Ju was poor," her father had said. "Too poor to support his mother, his wife, and his child. So he told his wife, 'The child is eating food my mother needs. Let us kill the child, for we can always have another, but if my mother dies, how could we replace her?'

"His wife did not dare contradict him and Guo Ju began to dig a grave. Suddenly, his spade struck a deeply buried vase which shattered, spilling hundreds of gold pieces, a gift from Heaven to Guo Ju, the filial son."

"What if there were no gold?" Lalu had asked.

"There was gold. More than enough for the rest of their lives," her father had said.

"But what if there wasn't?" Lalu insisted. "Would Guo Ju have killed his child?

"It's just a story from the Twenty-Four Legends of Filial Piety," her mother said. "To teach us we must honor our parents and do whatever we can to make their lives happy and comfortable."

"Would you kill me?"

Her father put down his half woven basket and pinched her cheek. "Of course not. Aren't you my qianjin, my thousand pieces of gold?" he asked.

And he had tickled her until she had laughed, "Yes, yes, yes."

Lalu splashed the rag she had just wrung out back into the icy water. She was being silly. What did that old story have to do with what was happening now? And anyway, hadn't the farmers just admitted that her father could be right? That he might succeed?

One farmer's voice rose above the others. "I can see Nathoy taking a chance with his savings, but to mortgage his farm too!"

"Good thing his daughter is so pretty."

"Mmm. Just the right age to fetch a good price."

"Don't be absurd. Nathoy wouldn't sell her. When his oldest girl died from small pox, he mourned her like a son."

"And when Pan lost all his pigs last year and wanted to sell his youngest girl to buy a new brood sow, Nathoy tried to talk him out of it."

"No, he would never sell his Lalu, his thousand pieces of gold."

"Did you ever think he would risk everything he has on a crop of winter wheat?"

TWO

The winter storm which had raged for almost a week, continued to rattle the paper that covered the windows. Rain, forced through the roof of straw and pine branches, pitted the dirt floor with little mud puddles. In the only lamp, a dish almost empty of bean oil, the flame sputtered, casting strange shadows.

Lalu, seated on her parents' heated brick bed, shivered. Her eyes were red and weepy from the smoke which filtered through the tunnels connecting the kitchen stove with the chimney, and she dropped her sewing to rub them.

Across the room, her mother knelt, stiff as stone, before the red gilt altar of Guanyin, the Goddess of Mercy. "Can the Goddess really save my father's wheat?" Lalu wondered.

Earlier, when her mother was lighting yet another stick of incense, Lalu had suggested that perhaps their village was too small and too far north for the gods to hear their prayers. Her mother had quickly knocked her head against the dirt floor, calling loudly on Heaven to ignore her daughter who should know better than to question the gods' supremacy and knowledge of everything that went on, even in the most faraway corners of China.

Then she had turned to Lalu and said, "We depend on Heaven and the Goddess Guanyin knows that. After all, it was she who took pity on the Han people when they were still living by hunting and gathering. When she saw how they suffered starvation because their ears of rice were empty, she went secretly into the fields and squeezed her breasts so her milk would flow into the ears of rice plants. Near the end, she had to press so hard that a mixture of milk and blood flowed into the plants, yet she did not stop until all the ears were filled."

Lalu stretched, careful not to disturb her two younger brothers who slept on either side of her. If she were a goddess like Guanyin, she would have filled the empty ears of rice with a mere flick of her wrist, and she would stop this storm at once and replant all of the wheat that had been destroyed or washed away. Then she would make the wheat harvest so plentiful that her father would be the richest man in the whole village. No, not just the village, but the whole district!

The door flew open, letting in a blast of wind and rain that gutted out the last glow of light. In the darkness, Lalu heard her mother rise and move, swift and sure-footed as a cat, into the kitchen. She felt a sudden sprinkle of water as her father shook off his straw rain cloak, letting it fall with a sodden rustle to the muddied floor. The smell of damp clothes mingled with the pungent odor of incense. Lalu sniffed. There was another smell, one of hot gaoliang wine. The kind her father offered to his dead parents and grandparents on feast days. The kind disappointed gamblers used to forget what they had lost.

Her mother returned and the room flared into light. Lalu blinked. Her father stood dripping in the middle of the room, his queue unraveled, his padded jacket and pants covered with mud and bits of wheat, broken twigs, and dead leaves.

"It's all gone," he said.

"Gone?" her mother echoed.

"Everything. Even what was set aside for the land tax."

"What will we do?" she whispered.

From where she huddled under the quilt, Lalu could see her mother's frightened whisper had shocked her father as much as herself. For until this moment, not once, even during the worst of times, had they glimpsed a shadow of doubt in her mother's belief that they would somehow survive.

Years ago, when her father had left for Manchuria, hoping to come back like Old Man Yang with a money belt full of gold, it was her mother who made her believe he would return even though every street in the village had at least one house where a husband, father, or son had gone into the barbaric North with hope, only to disappear forever. Then, during the year of famine after he returned, ragged and disappointed, her mother had quieted their terrible, gnawing hunger with little round bits of yeasty dough which swelled in their stomachs, giving them the illusion of fullness. And when they went into debt for a flock of brood hens and the bandits stole every one, her mother had merely pinched their solemn faces and said, "Heaven gave us life, Heaven will give us succor. We'll manage."

In every crisis, her mother's confident, "We'll manage," had brought them through. Why was she silent now?

"Mama?"

For a moment, before her mother turned and sank before the altar, their eyes locked, and in that brief instant, Lalu suddenly understood the reason for her mother's silence.

Before, they had somehow always scraped together the land tax. This time, with the farm so heavily mortgaged and the extra fields her father had leased, they could not. Unless. What was it the farmers had said? "Good thing his daughter is so pretty." "Just the right age to fetch a good price." Her father was going to sell her, and like Guo Ju's wife, her mother dared say nothing, for if her father did not pay the land tax, he would be sent to prison, and without him, the family would starve.

TWO

All Lalu's training in the four virtues of a woman told her she must accept the inevitable. She must be sold so the family could live. Nevertheless, her mind raced like a cornered rat searching for escape. There had to be some other way.

She crawled out from under the quilt. "We can sell the donkey," she suggested hopefully.

Her father sighed. "You don't know what you're talking about."

"If that's not enough, you can borrow the balance from Shi."

"Shi the Skin Tearer?" her father snapped bitterly. "How would I ever repay that blood sucker?"

Lalu swallowed. It was her life she was fighting for, and her father knew it. Why else was he allowing her to speak?

"You can let Chen, the laborer, go," she said.

"With all the extra fields I've leased? Impossible."

"A Cai can leave school to help."

"He's only eight, too small to do anything except children's work."

Lalu slipped off the bed and stood in front of her father. "I'm not too small. I'll work with you."

Her father brushed loose strands of hair from her forehead, his touch full of tender regret. "Qianjin, in this district women don't work in the fields. You know that."

"They do during harvest."

"That's different," he said heavily. "Only sons become farmers."

"I won't be a farmer, just your helper, and only until A Cai is bigger."

"We'd be the laughingstock of the whole village."

"We already are."

Immediately regretting her words, Lalu burrowed her head into her father's chest. Water squeezed from his rain-soaked clothes, spreading coldly over her, but she felt only the fierce pounding of his heart beneath her cheek.

"Baba, I beg you. Let me help you. I don't want to be..." She stopped, unable to say the word sold. "To go away," she finally whispered.

The muscles above her father's tightly clenched jaws quivered, and for a long moment there was only the sound of wind and rain.

"What about your golden lotus?" he asked.

Lalu released her father and stared down at her feet. Every day for two years, her mother had wound long white bandages around each foot in ever tightening bands, twisting her toes under her feet and forcing them back until her feet had become two dainty arcs. They were not as small or as beautiful as those of a girl from a wealthy family who would not need to use them at all. But they were useless for heavy labor.

Her mother rose and came to stand beside Lalu. "I'll unbind them."

"Is that possible?" her father stammered.

TWO

"We will make it possible," her mother said.

Later, in the quiet darkness of her own bed, Lalu dove under the quilt and felt her feet, no larger than a pair of newborn chicks. Dimly she remembered a time when her stride had been more than a few ladylike inches and she could run across the meadow, teasing a kite into the wind. Could her feet really become large and sturdy once again? Her hands curled around them, just as they had around the little featherless sparrow she had found last spring.

Her father had told her death was certain, and she should drown it so it would not suffer. Obediently she had plunged the tiny creature into a basin of water. Its beak opened and closed soundlessly as it struggled for air and its featherless wings pushed desperately against her clenched fists. She released the bird. But it was too late. Unable to rise above the surface of the water, its wild convulsions became shudders, and one by one, the ripples diminished until the water became as still as frozen ice.

Was it too late for her?

THREE

"Lalu," her father called.

Lalu straightened up from the row of millet she was thinning. She pulled her clinging, sweat-soaked jacket away from her body and wiped the perspiration from her face with her sleeve. Shading her eyes from the glare of the late afternoon sun, she looked over at her father.

"Take that bundle of firewood A Cai gathered to your mother," he said.

"I'll take it, Baba," A Cai said.

"No, this field must be finished today."

Each day her father searched for a new excuse to send her home early so she would not have to mix with the other farmers leaving the fields, and Lalu knew it was useless to offer to stay in her brother's place. Nevertheless, she tried. "A Cai is tired and I am not."

"Your mother needs you," he said tersely.

"Yes, Baba."

Pinching her brother's cheek sympathetically,

THREE

Lalu balanced her hoe and the bundle of firewood on top of the wheelbarrow and started down the terraced hillside to the village.

A colorful patchwork of green, brown, and yellow fields full of farmers with their sons and hired laborers stretched before her. Women washed clothes in the dikes by the willow-lined river bank, and old folks leaned against the levee walls, soaking up sunshine, talking story, and watching their grandchildren play around them. She could hear the laughter of small children, the cries of the peddlers shouting their wares; and when the breeze blew her way, she could smell the smoke that curled above the cluster of houses.

But it was what she could not see that showed the village as it really was. The oxen, mules, and donkeys kept well hidden for fear of bandit raids. The furrowed brows of wives gauging each meal's meager allotment so the carefully hoarded food might last until harvest. The knots of tension in the sun-blackened backs of farmers who knew that all their toil could be swept away in a moment, made futile by flood or drought or bandits or locusts.

From the time Lalu had learned to walk, she had worked: first, following her father's plow and dropping soy beans into the furrows; later, when her father planted the sweet potato vines, filling the holes with water, covering all but one leaf with soil; then, during the harvests, cleaning sweet potatoes for her mother to slice and dry, and picking peanuts off the vines. Even during the two years of foot-binding, when she could not walk, she had not been idle, learning to sew and spin and weave. And after her feet became little four-inch lotus, when she was no longer allowed to work in the fields, she had helped her mother at home. Except for the harvests. Then she and her mother joined the other women and girls, threshing wheat and millet, picking peanuts, and preparing sweet potatoes, turnips, cabbages, and other vegetables for storage. She had thought working as her father's laborer would be no harder. She had found she was wrong.

Her mother had tried to make unbinding Lalu's feet as easy as possible, loosening the bindings gradually, soaking, massaging, stuffing cotton between the toes so they could gradually expand outwards, but the toes had not flattened in time for spring planting. Chewing her lips to keep from crying, Lalu had carried heavy buckets of fertilizer into the fields, making her feet swell. Then, because her father had no stone roller to press the soil down so the young shoots would have solid earth for support, she had trampled the ground with her swollen feet. At night, when she took off the loosened bindings, the smell of decaying flesh had made her too ill to eat. But the ground for the peanut crop needed to be leveled and hardened; ridges had to be built up for planting the sweet potatoes; and the vegetable garden had to be laid out. Then the new seedlings had to be thinned and weeded; and always there was water to be carried up from the river. And when her mother, swollen with child again, neared her term, there were household chores as well, chores her parents said were not fitting for A Cai, a son.

Lalu now knew that her toes would never lie completely flat again, but callouses had formed; and though her walk was somewhat strange and rolling, she felt only pleasure in this her second year in the fields. She paid close attention when her father explained the proper way to fertilize a field or plant a sweet potato vine, feeling enormous pride as he entrusted her more and more with work that needed skillful, knowledgeable hands. There were even guilty moments when she was almost glad the wheat had failed, for she loved everything to do with farming: the preparation of the soil, the planting, the careful nurturing...

"Psssst."

Lalu jumped. A Cai leaped out from behind a grave mound and climbed onto the wheelbarrow, curling up behind the bundle of firewood.

"What?" Lalu began.

"I sneaked off and cut across the fields when Baba wasn't looking. Take me around behind the temple where he won't see me."

"You'd better hurry back before he misses you."

A Cai pouted. "I never get a chance to play with my friends."

Lalu tried to look stern, but his sweaty, dirt-streaked face and babyish pout made the corners of her mouth twitch. "Baba will be furious."

"You can make it all right with him, you always do."

She laughed, knowing her little brother had gotten the better of her again. "Okay, hang on tight!" she cried. And she raced down the hill in her strange, rolling lope, the wheelbarrow hurtling noisily over the bumps, her long, thick braid flying straight out behind.

Lalu, exhilarated from her run, burst through the door, panting. Her mother, face moist and red from the steaming kettles, broke off the folk song she was humming to A Da, the baby strapped on her back.

"Did I see A Cai behind the temple?" she asked.

"He's tired," Lalu defended.

Her mother fed the fire with gaoliang stalks. "But not too tired to play with his friends. You spoil him."

A Fa toddled in from the courtyard. He tugged at Lalu's pants. "Mama has a surprise for you."

Lalu swung her little brother up and hugged him. She pinched his legs which protruded from split pants. "Hmmm, you're getting fat, fat enough to eat," she said, taking a playful bite.

"Come see!" he demanded, kicking.

She set him down. "See what?"

THREE

"Over here, look."

He pulled her out into the courtyard and pointed to the wooden table set for two. "You're going to eat with Baba from now on. Mama said so."

Like all the other men, Lalu's father was fed first, before his wife and children, and with the better food. As a child, Lalu had asked why, and her mother had explained, "Men are the pillars of the family. We depend on them for our lives, so they must be fed well." Now she, Lalu, was to eat first too!

Her eyes brimmed with tears. It didn't matter that the farmers said her father was turning Heaven and earth upside down by allowing his daughter to work by his side. Or that their wives told her mother, "Your daughter's face is passable, but those big feet are laughable." Or that A Cai's friends called her a carp on herring feet, and her own friends avoided her. Her parents understood!

"What's wrong? Aren't you happy" A Fa demanded.

"Leave your sister alone," their mother said. She turned to Lalu. "Come inside, I have something to show you before your father gets home."

A Fa waddled ahead importantly. Their mother pulled a stool out from under the table and set A Fa on it.

"You stay here and keep the flies off the pickles and salt fish," she told him.

Lalu, dazed with pride and joy, followed her

mother inside. Her mother reached into the clothing box and took out a small, fitted under jacket, the kind women wore to flatten their breasts.

"I made this for you."

Lalu blushed. "I don't need it yet."

"You're fourteen, a woman. Look how your sweaty outer jacket clings to you. Do you want to be called a wanton?"

Lalu held the under jacket up against her. "It's too small."

"Try it on," her mother said.

"Now?"

"Now."

Lalu turned to face the wall. Her whole body afire with embarrassment, she unbuttoned her loose-fitting cotton jacket, slipped it off, and struggled into the tight-fitting bodice her mother had made.

"I can't breathe."

"Nonsense, it's perfect," her mother said, tugging it in place.

"How will I swing my hoe?"

Her mother sighed. "The villagers are right. We should have sold you."

"No, Mama. You don't mean that."

As though Lalu were a child again, her mother pulled Lalu's outer jacket over the bodice. "Don't you know I say that for your sake, not mine?" she scolded gently. "If we had sold you, we would have found you a good mistress, one not too far away, and you would be doing decent woman's work in a good household, not bitter labor."

"But I love working in the fields," Lalu protested.

"And when you became of age, your mistress would have found you a good husband, and you would have been free again. Now you're neither snake nor dragon. You are a woman, yet you work like a man, a laborer. Who will marry you?"

"I don't care. I'm happy, really I am."

"You're a woman. You should be growing sons, not vegetables."

"I will, just as soon as A Cai is old enough to really help."

"If it were only that easy," her mother said. "Have you forgotten the saying — A large footed woman tarries, for no one wants to marry her?"

"But you said you would rebind my feet," Lalu stammered.

"I will, but they're ruined. They'll never have the same perfect shape or be as small. Besides, it's not just your feet. You're doing what no woman in this village, this district, has done, and your name is on every gossip's tongue. What decent, modest woman will take you for a daughter-in-law now?"

FOUR

Five years' labor in the fields had given Lalu the experienced eyes of a skilled farmer and she knew as soon as she began spreading the sweet potatoes on the kitchen floor that Old Man Yang had cheated them. Three baskets of undersized and half-rotted sweet potatoes in exchange for a healthy, hard-working donkey! But, in the beginning of the third year of drought, with the mortgage still unpaid, and everything else of value either sold or stolen by bandits, there had been no other way to get the seed potatoes they needed for spring planting. Grimly, she began sorting them into two piles. The better ones for seed. The others to help eke out their diet of dry roots and watery gruel.

Outside, deep-toned drums throbbed like thunder, and Lalu knew without looking that the village leaders were, once again, carrying the Dragon King into the fields to show him the earth, parched and cracked from the angry sun. For two springs and summers they had watched helplessly as the river shriveled into a shallow stream and then a trickle, forcing them to dig deeper and deeper for water. Last year, when the wood buckets dipped into the riverbed began to fill with mud, the village leaders had carried the Dragon King into the fields to show him the stunted crops with deformed, twisted leaves. Men and boys with wreaths of coarse grass on their heads had followed, beating drums and bearing banners inscribed with prayers for rain. The Dragon King had sent no rain then. What made anyone think he would send rain now?

Lalu's stomach gnawed hungrily. She kneaded it, but it only grew more demanding. She picked up another sweet potato and examined it. It already had toothmarks from a rat. Two. If she took a bite, a small one, surely no one would know. Trancelike, she lifted the potato to her open mouth, but before she could bite into it, a drop of saliva fell on it, darkening the skin like blood. She hurled it to the floor. How could she even think of satisfying her own hunger when everyone else in her family was starving?

She rose and opened the door. Dry heat hit her with the force of a blow and she leaned weakly against the door post. The sun-faded strips of red and black New Year greetings crackled beneath her weight, crumbling into dust, and Lalu jerked straight, relieved her mother was not home to witness such a bad omen.

Her eyes adjusted to the glare, and she saw her

father, A Cai, and a few other farmers break off
from the tail end of the procession returning to the
temple. She knew she would not be permitted to
join them, but perhaps she could get close enough to
hear what they might say. Anything, rather than
hold potatoes she could not eat. She banged the
door shut and walked toward them.

Heat enveloped her like a thick winter quilt, and
her feet scuffed up clouds of dust, clogging her
nostrils, making her eyes smart. By the time she
neared the temple, her hair and clothes were sticky
with sweat. She thought of her mother's face when
A Fa had suggested they water the fields by
wringing their sweat-drenched clothes over the
dying crops. At the time it had made Lalu giggle,
but now, as she crouched down behind the temple
wall, she did not even smile. The situation was too
grave.

"We must go to the main river for water," she
heard her father say.

"But that's over the mountain, half-a-day's
journey away," Old Man Yang protested.

"It's the only way," her father insisted.

"Full of ideas aren't you?" the old man said.

"Yes, like winter wheat," someone chortled.

"And making a girl work like a man!"

The farmers, eager for something to laugh at,
exploded in a roar.

"This time Nathoy is right. We cannot wait and
hope any longer," someone interrupted.

FOUR

"We could try going to the main river," another voice grudgingly agreed.

"What about bandits?"

Lalu felt her sweat turn cold. Ever since she could remember, the village had been threatened by bandits, but since the drought, they had grown in numbers. The raids had been more frequent, and many of the bandits were former laborers who had lived and worked in the village. They knew what to look for and where to find it. And they were completely ruthless.

"Why would they attack us?" her father asked. "We'll be carrying nothing but our buckets."

"They might kidnap one of us for ransom," Old Man Yang suggested.

"Except for yourself, who has money?"

"When they discovered the Pans were too poor to pay a ransom for their father, they made the old man dig his own grave and lie in it. Then they bashed in his skull with the shovel."

"And when Shi was slow paying the ransom for his son, the bandits sliced off the boy's ear."

"It's the women and children I'm worried about. If they're left alone, who knows what we'll find when we return."

"We could take turns going. That way, there would always be men in the village."

"Just having men here is not enough. We must fight them," Lalu's father urged.

"Didn't you see what happened to Fat Wu?"

Everyone grew silent, for Fat Wu had leaped at a bandit's throat only to have his head severed in a single blow. The head had rolled into the gutter and down the street, knocking against sudden curves, splattering blood against courtyard walls until another bandit swooped on it and pierced it with a pole which he stabbed into the ground. The mouth had hung open and the big white teeth had gleamed ghostlike in the predawn darkness while his queue, matted with blood, swayed fitfully back and forth, a warning to anyone else foolish enough to resist.

Lalu's father broke the silence. "Fat Wu tried to fight them alone. We must organize into teams and patrol the streets and lanes."

"Wasn't it your idea to have soldiers come help us? They were worse than the bandits."

"The ones billeted with us ate everything we'd been able to save from the bandits."

"And I was afraid to leave my wife and daughters alone for even a minute the whole time they were here!"

"It's you and your mad schemes that have brought us all this bad luck!" Old Man Yang accused.

"Don't be so foolish," Lalu's father said.

"Look who dares call us foolish."

A shrill, inhuman scream, more terrible than anything Lalu had ever heard, ripped through the cluster of farmers like a crack of lightning, followed by a second, even more piercing, shriek and a rumble like thunder.

Lalu's head jerked up. A thick ochre haze was hurtling down the mountainside toward the village.

"Bandits!"

The farmers scattered, racing for their homes and hiding places. Lalu, her legs weak from months of hunger and cramped from squatting, limped after them. Grit from the swirling dust burned her eyes and rasped down her throat. She covered her face with her hands and struggled on blindly.

A glancing blow knocked her flat. Crawling to her knees, she gaped at the horse that blocked her path. It was the big, handsome stallion A Gao's father had purchased the year of the good harvest. How she had admired its strength and beauty! Now it shook and whimpered above her like a frightened colt. Where his big brown eyes had been were two bloody holes. A long needle, the kind used for making shoes, protruded from the left hole.

A Gao came up from behind and made a grab for the halter. The horse circled crazily, kicking and screaming.

"Help me," A Gao pleaded.

"How could you?" Lalu gasped.

"I had to," he cried, tears streaming down his face. "You know the bandits only take good horses. This way he'll be blind, but he'll still be ours."

"You blundering idiot," A Gao's father panted as he tried to corner the animal. "I told you to tether him tightly."

He leaped up, snatched the needle and hurled it, dripping, onto the ground. The horse screamed and reared, his hooves beating a staccato tattoo against the courtyard walls. Lalu tried to roll away, but the bloodied pits held her in their grip.

"Come on," A Gao said, dragging Lalu to her feet. "The bandits are at the edge of town already."

FIVE

The bedlam inside the house restored Lalu to reality. Their mother, with the newest baby strapped to her back, was throwing sweet potatoes into a basket, half dragging A Da who clung wailing to the hem of her pants. A Fa trailed after them, alternately trying to get their mother's attention and chew on a potato their mother had dropped.

"There's no time to take the little ones away. You'll all have to hide in the fertilizer pit," her father ordered.

Lalu, frantically helping her mother scoop up the sweet potatoes, protested. "There's no room."

"What if the babies cry?" her mother added.

"You'll just have to make sure they don't," he said, hurrying them into the courtyard.

Flies buzzed furiously as A Cai helped their mother and the baby into the pit. He passed A Da and A Fa down to her, then Lalu and the basket of sweet potatoes. Finally, A Cai squeezed into the crowded hole. Manure and refuse swilled around their ankles. Flies wriggled in and out of their ears and nostrils.

"It stinks," A Fa complained.

"That's what makes it a good hiding place," their mother said. "A Cai, you're too tall. Crouch down."

"There's no room."

"Everyone move back so A Cai can squat."

"He's sitting in shit," A Fa giggled.

"Shh or the bandits will steal you away forever."

"Lalu, rest your basket of potatoes on A Cai so you can carry A Da," their mother said.

"Wait, I'm losing my balance."

The basket slipped and the potatoes slid and plopped into the murky mess. The flies nearest the bottom rose in noisy spirals, causing the ones above to whir and thrum against the closely huddled bodies.

"I told you to wait," A Cai snapped.

A Fa began to cry. "That's the only basket we brought. What will we eat?"

"Never mind," their mother soothed. "We'll fish them out and wash them off."

"I won't eat shit," A Fa sobbed.

A Da started to cry.

"Quiet," their mother commanded in a hoarse whisper. "You'll start the baby crying, and believe me, if the bandits find us, you won't need to worry about eating."

"But I'm hungry," A Fa whined.

"Me too," A Da lisped between wails.

"Listen. If you promise to stop crying, I'll bring the other basket," Lalu said.

The children quieted immediately.

"There's no time," their mother said. "I can hear the bandits chopping in doors already."

The children began to snivel.

"I'll go," A Cai sighed, trying to raise himself.

"You're wedged in," Lalu said, hoisting herself up and out of the pit. She leaned over. "Remember, you must be quiet or I won't come back."

She ran across the courtyard and into the house. Her father was putting the last potatoes into a basket. "What are you doing?"

"The potatoes we had fell into the manure," Lalu said breathlessly. The boisterous clamor outside grew louder. She reached for the basket. "Here, I'll take these back."

"No, we must have something to give the bandits or they'll tear the place apart."

"The children are crying. Let me take a few to quiet them."

Her father scooped up two handfuls and threw them into the apron of Lalu's jacket. She turned to run. Bang! The door shook, showering dust and bits of thatch onto Lalu and her father.

"Open up!" a voice roared above the clatter of hoofbeats, splintering wood, and terrified screaming.

"Quick, behind the stove," her father said.

Lalu scrambled up, the potatoes dropping and

rolling across the floor as she squeezed into the narrow crevice. Through a crack, she saw the door burst open and a bandit stride in, kicking aside the splintered crossbar.

"What are you hiding?" he demanded.

"Nothing. See, I've gathered some sweet potatoes for you," Lalu's father said, thrusting the basket toward him.

The bandit's knife slashed the basket from his hands and potatoes spilled all across the floor. "You dare insult me with one basket!"

"It's all we have left."

"Liar!"

Lalu shrank against the wall as the bandit knocked her father aside. Breaking pots, smashing crockery, and upsetting baskets, he strode across the trail of manure to the back of the stove where she hid.

Rough hands yanked Lalu out and threw her down.

Her father bent to help her. "That's my daughter."

The bandit kicked her father across the room. "I know," he leered, jerking Lalu off the floor.

She kicked and drummed her fists against him, but he overpowered her easily, trapping her legs between his and pinning her arms against his side, hugging her to him. She sank her teeth into his arm. He laughed and twisted his arm free, then snapped her jaws between his fingers and forced her to face him. She stared defiantly, screwing up her nose at his stale garlic breath.

His small, sharp eyes glittered. "Don't recognize me, do you?"

The voice was disturbingly familiar. She looked more closely at the swarthy face that loomed above her. Black eyes and long nose were embedded in greasy, pockmarked skin. Stiff black hairs formed a scraggly, off-kilter mustache and beard that hid twisted, misshapen lips. Shave his forehead, comb the hair into a neat queue, take away the mustache and beard, and he would look just like her father's old laborer, the one who had worked for them the year of the winter wheat.

"Chen," she breathed.

"Smart as well as fierce!" he roared.

Her father rose. "Let her go!" he commanded.

"Careful how you speak to me, I'm not your laborer anymore."

Her father stepped forward, raising clenched fists.

"Let's not have any foolish show of bravery," Chen sneered. "A single whistle and my men will come pouring through that door and smash you to pulp, just like this."

Dragging Lalu with him, he swiftly stamped the sweet potatoes until the floor was caked with rusty red smears.

Angry tears spurted down Lalu's cheeks. "How

can you, a farmer, do such a terrible thing?" she cried.

"Quite easily," he said, his voice as cold and sharp as the edge of the knife he held. "I never was a farmer. Only a hired laborer. Someone to get rid of when times are bad. But now I'm a bandit leader. Boss of fifty men."

Out of the corner of her eye, Lalu saw her father reaching stealthily for the sickle. At the same instant, Chen knocked it out of reach.

"You just don't understand, do you? A single whistle. A shout. And your wife and children will be worse than dead. Remember, I know your hiding places." He kicked meaningfully at the closest glob of manure. "Even if I didn't, your little fox has left a trail a blind man can follow."

Lalu's father sank to his knees. "Please, I beg you. Let her go."

"Don't worry, I'll pay you for this little fox."

Lalu gasped.

"She's not for sale," her father said. But his sagging shoulders betrayed defeat.

Lalu stiffened, refusing to give in as easily. She had persuaded her father to allow her to work in the fields, she would persuade Chen not to take her.

"Think of your wife and children," she said.

Chen's knife blade grazed Lalu's neck as he snapped her head back with a yank of her braid. "Did your father think of them when he took away my livelihood?"

Lalu bit her lip. She shouldn't have mentioned his family, but it was too late to back down. "There are other farmers to work for."

"Not since the drought."

"We've been hungry too. The younger children are covered with sores and their stomachs are bloated like dead fish."

"But you're alive. My wife and children are dead. From starvation."

"I didn't know."

"Of course not," Chen lashed. "Who cares about a common laborer?"

He burst into ugly laughter, splattering Lalu with a spray of saliva. "Do you really think a sentimental fool can be a bandit chief? When the drought came, I joined the bandits and led a raid on my own village. Sold my children and gave my wife to the rest of the men to use. That's why they made me chief."

He held Lalu at arm's length, examining her like a farmer about to purchase livestock. "Pretty face. Nice white teeth and shiny hair. But such big feet! The brothels in Shanghai like bound feet and smooth white skin. You are burned black." He smiled lasciviously. "Of course, my men wouldn't care. You could be a common wife to them. My wife lasted a week. But you're tough. I'm sure you'd last at least a month." He nuzzled his scratchy beard against her cheek. "Then again, maybe I'll keep you for myself."

Lalu heard her father groan. She gritted her teeth, determined not to show her fear.

Chen raised his head and shouted. "Zhuo."

A short, stocky bandit filled the gaping hole where the door had been.

"Bring me some seed."

Almost immediately, Zhuo returned with two small bags no larger than Lalu's fists. Chen took the bags. "Round up the men and bring me my horse," he ordered.

He threw a bag in front of Lalu's father. It burst, scattering soybeans.

Lalu stared at her father, willing him not to pick them up. He reached out, hesitated, then looked up at Lalu, his eyes pleading for understanding. She twisted her face away, a sob strangling in her throat. Behind her, she heard him snatch the bag and scoop up the spilled seed.

"Two bags," her father begged. "She's worth two bags of seed."

Laughing scornfully, Chen tossed the other bag down, flung Lalu over his shoulder like a side of pork, and stalked out the door.

SIX

The bandits rode silently, in single file, sometimes allowing the horses to walk, other times breaking into a trot, and occasionally, for no apparent reason, beating the horses into a gallop. Lalu's eyes smarted and teared from the gritty, yellow gray dust that swirled around them. Squeezed between Chen and the pommel of the wooden saddle, her pants rubbed like sandstone between her legs where the soft inner flesh of her thighs had scraped raw from the long ride. She strained forward, her collar chafing painfully where Chen's knife had grazed her neck. A long, low branch whipped against her. The horse stumbled and a bolt of fire shot up Lalu's spine. She bit her lip, tasting blood.

Long after she thought she could not bear the torment another moment, they halted. Chen dismounted and Lalu sagged with relief. Behind her, she heard the other bandits dismount, the sounds of snapping branches and brush being dragged.

The arrogance with which they left her mounted and free to kick her horse into a gallop depressed Lalu more than if she had been tied and heavily guarded, for it confirmed what she already knew. Escape was hopeless. Earlier, she had tried to keep track of landmarks. While there was still some light and they were covering familiar ground, she had been able to tag unusual rock formations, trees, and mountains. But since they had entered strange territory and dusk had deepened into night, it had become impossible. Besides, even if she did somehow elude her captors and find her way home, her parents would not dare take her back. She had not been kidnapped. She had been sold. She belonged to Chen.

A flash of light followed by a burst of flames lit the darkness and Lalu saw the broken columns of a ruined temple. In the distance she saw another fire flare. Seconds later, a third fire sparked on the horizon. Was this some strange bandit ritual of thanksgiving? Then where was their sacrifice?

She trembled as Chen and his men let out a roar and rushed toward her, their faces ghostly pale in the flickering light. She kicked the horse. It reared, and she felt herself tossed into the darkness.

Oblivion, as sweetly warm and comforting as her mother's arms, embraced Lalu. Harsh shouts pricked the edges of her consciousness. Unwilling to give up the peace that had spread like liquid warmth through her tortured limbs, Lalu resisted until stinging slaps and punches pried her eyes open.

She expected a ring of faces. But there was only one. Chen's. The other men were already mounted, restless, eager to leave. Lalu felt foolish relief. The bandits had been rushing for their horses, not for her. The fires were not a religious rite, but beacons to guide them.

"You stupid whore, you could have damaged my horse," Chen snapped, flinging Lalu over the saddle. "If my men didn't need a woman, I'd kill you."

So he had already decided to give her to his men, Lalu thought dully. What was it he had said? "You could be a common wife to them. My wife lasted a week. But you're tough. I'm sure you'd last at least a month." What did he mean?

Dimly she remembered a night as a child when she had wakened to strange, muffled sounds from her parents' room. Frightened, she had leaped out of bed and run to them.

From the doorway, she saw the darkness of her father's larger bulk heave, panting, against her mother, who, flattened against the bed, moaned, then issued the short, sharp cry of a wounded bird.

Lalu scrambled up onto the bed, beating her fists against her father, sobbing, "Leave Mama alone."

Her mother grabbed Lalu's arms and ordered her back to her own bed.

"But he was hurting you," Lalu cried.

Her mother had pushed her away. "You're too young to understand."

Now, years later, she still did not really understand. Vaguely she realized that what her parents did at night was not unlike the coupling that occurred between animals. No one talked about it directly, but from the accumulated knowledge gleaned from years of whispers, she sensed it was something that was all right if it happened between husband and wife, shameful and terrible if the man and woman were not married.

Nevertheless, it happened. In places called brothels. During bandit raids. Sometimes with soldiers quartered in the village. And once, she had heard her mother and some of her friends whispering about a neighbor who had suddenly vanished because she had "disgraced" herself.

Lalu blushed hotly, remembering the time she had studied two dogs locked together. The male had mounted the female. She had quivered dreadfully, but she had not died. Did Chen's wife die because there were fifty men, not one? Then how did women in the brothels survive? Surely they coupled with more than that. Was there something bandits did that made it worse?

After Pan's wife was used by a bandit, she had hung herself. Everyone agreed she had done the proper thing, and her husband had built a paifang to commemorate her courage and virtue. Should she try to kill herself? Was that what Chen's wife had done? Then why had she waited a week? And why did Chen think she, Lalu, would last a month?

She knew it was important for her to sort it all out and try to make sense of it. But her head throbbed from the constant jolting. Her throat demanded water. And her body, exhausted beyond endurance, cried for sleep. Strange night noises were an added distraction. She cocked her ear. Was a wild animal crashing through the under- growth? Or more than one? From the amount of noise, it sounded like a pack. She glanced up at Chen. It was too dark to see much more than shadow, but he seemed unconcerned, letting the tired horses make their own pace.

Suddenly, there was a rush of dark shadows and excited shouts as bandits greeted cohorts left be- hind to light the beacons. Lalu clutched the pommel.

"What took so long?"

"We thought the devil had snared you."

"So, you captured a goddess."

"More like a whore!"

The men's voices blared like thunder claps in the quiet of the night. Chen shouted above the hubub. "Silence until we reach camp!"

Immediately, the men stopped their excited talk and only the rhythmic drumming of hoofbeats, the chatter of cicadas, and the hum of an occasional mosquito broke the silence as they headed toward the third beacon.

Lalu had supposed the third fire marked the camp, but it did not. Again, there was a burst of excitement as the bandits greeted each other, and again, Chen ordered the men silent. She was amazed at the way the bandits obeyed him. Obviously his command was absolute. If he decided to take her for himself, surely the men would not dare contradict or disobey. Wouldn't that be better than being thrown like a piece of meat to a pack of starving beasts? And if Chen kept her for himself, wouldn't they be husband and wife?

Her stomach rebelled at the thought of such an ugly old man for a groom. But hadn't her mother warned her that no decent family would take her for a daughter-in-law? That was why, at eighteen, when all her friends were already mothers, she remained unmarried. Unwanted. Besides, even good matches did not guarantee good husbands. Marriage brokers often lied, and everyone knew of girls who thought the red chair was carrying them to rich households with young, handsome husbands only to find they had been cheated.

How would Chen treat her? The winter he had lived with them as her father's laborer, he had never come back from market without a sweetmeat for her and her brother. In the evenings, he had often whittled little toy animals for them or woven delicate balls out of straw, all the time holding them

spellbound with marvelous stories of mighty war-
riors and vengeful ghosts. But he had changed.
Sold his own children and caused his wife's death.
Still, her mother said if a woman were clever, she
could persuade a man to do her will. Could she win
Chen over, entice him to be kind?

Lalu swallowed hard and leaned back, soft and
cuddly, against Chen. Tilting her face up, she
whispered. "Let me be yours."

His hand slid under her jacket, deftly unhooking
the buttons on her tight inner bodice. He fondled her
breasts. Instinctively, she stiffened. Desperately,
she tried to relax. Instead, she felt a rush of
goosebumps and a burning redness sweep over
her. She forced her body, however unyielding, to
remain pressed against him.

Chen twisted her nipple cruelly. "I'm not so
easily fooled, Little Sister," he said, withdrawing
his hand.

Tears of humiliation coursed down Lalu's
cheeks. "I'm a farmer, not a wanton," she wanted
to cry. "Then act like a farmer," a voice inside her
said. When bandits, insects, disease, rain, or
drought wiped out a crop, a farmer did not crumple
and cry like a disappointed child, he began the
whole process of fertilizing, plowing, and reseeding
once again. Even now, with the drought into its
third year, the farmers in her village remained
undefeated, searching for ways to save their land
and their families. Could she do any less? The seed

from her sale would save her father's land and her
mother and brothers from starvation. Now she had
to save herself.

She would find a way to escape. Not back to her
village, she knew she could never go home again,
but to a large town or city where the bandits would
never find her.

SEVEN

Lalu wakened feeling stiff and sore. She stretched. Her arms and legs hit sharp edges. Puzzled, she opened her eyes. She was wedged in by bags, boxes, baskets, and trunks. She reached out to push them aside, then froze as events from the day before crowded in on her: the raid, her sale, her failure to please Chen, their noisy arrival in camp, Chen's orders to dump her with the rest of the booty in this long, windowless room.

She remembered fighting to stay awake as the narrow room filled with fierce-looking camp dogs and men pushing and shoving and all talking at once. The barking and shouting giving way to sounds of eating. And, finally, the agonizing fragrance of the bandits' dinner forcing her to give in to her exhaustion as a means of escape. How long had she slept? Was she alone? Cautiously, Lalu raised herself so she could see beyond the boxes and trunks that surrounded her.

Through a curtain of sickeningly sweet smoke,

she sighted half-naked men stretched in pairs on long sleeping platforms on either side of her. They lay facing each other. Beneath each pair, she saw a small, lighted peanut oil lamp, partly covered with a paper shade. Over the flame, each man held a long, slender wooden pipe with a softly spluttering mass in the bowl. As the dark brown lumps became smaller, the smokers reshaped them into cones and resumed smoking. Lalu's pulse quickened. Concentrating on their pipes, the bandits took no more notice of her than they did of the dogs gnawing on leftover bones. This was her chance to escape.

Her eyes searched the smoke-blackened walls for a door, finding one behind her, to the left, not more than five feet away. Unguarded. She started to climb over the trunks and boxes.

A glitter of gold stopped her. She leaned down to grab it, but it was only a character painted on a red leather trunk. Disappointed, she pushed aside a basket of turnips and squeezed between two boxes. Midway she twisted back to stare at the painted gold. Though she could not read, she knew this pair of characters. Everyone did. Double happiness, the characters used for weddings. This was a wedding trunk, and a wedding trunk meant jewelry, jewelry she needed to exchange for food or pawn for cash.

Lalu crouched beside the trunk. Padlocked. In one swift motion, she removed the brass earring from her left lobe, straightened it, and picked at the clasp. The smoke and shaded lamps made it hard to see clearly, and she fumbled. The lock slipped in her sweaty palms. She wiped her hands dry on her jacket and probed deeper. The earring stuck inside the clasp. She pulled. It would not yield. She twisted it and pulled again, but the end of the straightened earring was too short and thin for her to get a proper grip. Head throbbing and mouth dry, she leaned down, gripped the sliver of wire with her teeth, and pulled.

The wire yanked free, springing the lock. At the same time, the force threw Lalu against a basket which tumbled, scattering peanuts with a loud, dry rustle. The bandits did not look up from their pipes, but the dogs trotted over and sniffed at the peanuts and Lalu. Scarcely daring to breathe, she waited for the dogs to go back to their bones, then pried open the lid.

The trunk was filled with silks and satins. A wealthy bride. She felt around the sides and all along the bottom for jewelry. Nothing. Was she wasting precious time searching for what might not be there? No. She must find jewelry. If not in this trunk, then in another, for without it, she would be helpless, the prey of charletans as evil as these bandits.

Lalu plunged back into the jumble of jackets, skirts, and trousers, tossing out garment after garment until the trunk gaped empty. Nothing. Dizzy with disappointment, she fell back. Something sharp pricked through her thin cotton pants. She pulled it out tiredly and threw it into the empty trunk. It winked up at her. Gold! A gold earring.

She snatched it up and felt around the mess of clothing for its mate. Wildly hurling garments back into the trunk, her fingers knocked against something cold and round. A jade bangle. A silver hairpin. The mate for the gold earring. And three jade buttons. Shaking with relief, Lalu used the earrings and hairpin to hook the bangle and buttons to the wide inside waistband of her pants. She pulled her jacket down over her cache, took one last glance at the bandits, and headed for the door.

The weakness in her legs and the hollow cramping in her stomach reminded Lalu she had not eaten since the bowl of thin gruel at breakfast the day before. She pushed the thought from her mind. She must leave while she still had the chance. Later, when she was safe, she would eat. She edged forward, leaning against the trunks and boxes, grateful for their support. A haze of black and red dots thickened and came together in a solid sheet of black. She shook her head impatiently. For a moment, the darkness faded. Then again it deepened. Tears of frustration pricked Lalu's eyelids. She must eat now.

Sinking to the floor, she searched for some leftover she could grab without upsetting the dogs. As her fingers touched the rim of a bowl, her mouth flooded with saliva. She lifted the bowl to her lips and shoveled in scraps of pork and congealed millet, barely chewing before she swallowed and gulped some more.

Suddenly, the bowl was wrenched from her grasp. She thought at first that the hideous beast who had seized it was a dog, but bony talons clutched the bowl. Could the long tangled hair and matted beard be covering a man? Repelled yet unable to move, she watched the creature lick the bowl clean and hobble away on all fours, dragging a chain and iron weight which left a deep groove in the dirt floor.

"How do you like our bear?"

Lalu whirled around. A small, slightly built man with hollow eyes and sunken cheeks dropped down lightly from the sleeping platform beside her. How long had he been watching? Did he guess she was heading for the door and escape?

He came closer. She must distract him. Talk.

"It's not a bear, it's a man," she said, trying to keep her voice low and steady.

"Once, maybe, but he's been our bear for years. Keeps us entertained with his dancing and tricks during the long winter months when we're snowed in. Of course, we won't need him now that we've got you."

Lalu forced a laugh. "Me?"

"We've drawn lots to see who will get you first. Worst luck I'm forty-three." He lunged and grabbed her to him. "Unless..."

The door burst open. "Soldiers!" the man silhouetted in the doorway shouted. In the rush of stampeding bandits, Lalu found herself seized by a medium-sized, middle-aged man with a long, droopy gray mustache. She dug her heels into the dirt.

"Let me go," she begged.

He hoisted her off the floor. "Believe me, you're better off with us than the soldiers," he said.

Wedged tightly between the bandit who held her and the pommel of the saddle, Lalu listened to the scouts' report. There were soldiers everywhere, they said. And those sons of turtles looked as though they intended to stay.

"This fit of housecleaning won't last. It never does," Chen said.

"What do we do until they leave?" his second-in-command asked.

"Gao and Ma have camps near here. We can take refuge with them," Chen said.

"Wu's camp is not too far either," a tall, thin man added.

"Take some men with you and go see what the situation is with them," Chen ordered. He pointed to a dense thicket about half a li away. "We'll wait for you there."

The trees sheltered them from the glare of the hot afternoon sun, but not from the mosquitoes and horseflies. The horses, nostrils quivering, tossed their heads and flicked their tails, but their necks, legs, and bellies were soon covered with bites. Lalu felt welts rising wherever her skin was exposed. She slapped and scratched until her fingers became sticky with blood, but the itching and irritating buzzing did not stop.

She studied the bandits, wondering if she could crawl away unnoticed. Splotches of blood and flattened insects flecked their backs and faces which glistened with huge blisters of sweat. They swore and slapped themselves angrily.

"A fire would get rid of those blood suckers."

"And bring the soldiers down on us like maggots."

"If they're not deaf, you ignorant bastard, they can hear the horses stamping and snorting."

"But you can see smoke farther away."

"They might think the smoke is from a soldier camp."

"And what do we do if they come? Serve hot wine?"

Chen turned to the bandit who had seized Lalu when the soldiers came. "Ding, build a fire."

"It's too hot," Ding grumbled.

Lalu jumped to her feet. She would quiet Ding's suspicions by gathering brush from nearby, then go farther and farther until she was safely hidden in the forest. "I'll help," she said.

Chen kicked her to the ground. "And fly the coop and spoil our fun?"

The men laughed.

A heavy-set man threw himself on top of her. "How about a taste of swan's meat?" he sneered, ripping the buttons off her jacket.

Lalu struggled, but against his bulk she was helpless. The sharp points from the earrings hidden in her waistband dug into her belly and she felt a strange hardness swell and press against her thigh.

"Get off," she gasped.

"And lose the chance to eat a virgin?" he grinned, his calloused fingers tearing at her flesh.

"Hey, Zhuo, get off her. My number is before yours!" Ding protested.

"Mine too!" another bandit added.

The two men fell on Zhuo, pulling him off Lalu.

"Zhu drew the lowest number, he goes first," Ding said.

"He's with the scouts," Zhuo protested. "I say we draw lots again."

"And lose my low number? Never." Ding laughed scornfully. "You're just afraid that by the time you get her she'll be like a mushy old sweet potato, too much for someone like you with testicles the size of a gnat."

Zhuo sprang to his feet and lunged at Ding. "I'll tear your tongue out, you son of a whore."

Chen jumped between them. "Get the fire

going before the horses bleed to death," he snapped. "The lottery stands as it is."

The scouts returned with the first evening star.
Even before they dismounted, Lalu knew from their
faces that the situation was desperate. She felt a
small flutter of hope. If the news was bad for the
bandits, it might be good for her.

"Our rice is cooked," Zhu reported. "Wu's camp
is deserted. Ma is taking his men up into Mongolia.
And Gao's band, poor bastards, must have been
taken by surprise. They're all dead."

"We'll hole up in Shanghai," Chen decided.

"With soldiers crawling all over, we can't make
any raids. How will we eat?" his second-in-command
asked.

"We'll sell the whore." Without pausing for
discussion or argument, Chen continued, "There'll
be less chance of getting caught if we travel in
smaller groups." Swiftly, he selected four bandits
to act as leaders and began dividing the men among
them.

"Come here, Little Sister," Ding hissed.

Lalu did not move.

"Come here," Ding repeated more urgently. He
edged closer. "Ride with me. I can help you."

Lalu tightened her grip on her torn jacket.
"Like you did when you brought me here?"

"You have to trust me. It will be days before we reach Shanghai and you will need my help. Like you did with Zhuo just now."

He had helped her when Zhuo jumped her, Lalu admitted. And later, waiting for the scouts to return, he had stayed close, watching. She had thought he had been watching to see she did not escape. Now she wondered.

"The whore will ride with me," Chen said.

Ding jerked Lalu toward him. "Save yourself the discomfort," he said obsequiously. "I'll make sure our little bag of gold doesn't get lost."

"Or damaged!" Chen warned, laughing.

"Or damaged," Ding agreed, dragging Lalu to the tree where his horse waited.

EIGHT

They traveled hard, following narrow deer paths that ran along ridges and sides of mountains, making endless ascents and descents to avoid villages, military forts, and camps, stopping only when the horses were too exhausted to go any further. Then, while the horses grazed, the bandits, edgy, fatigued, and chronically hungry, vented their frustrations by baiting Lalu. But when they became rough or tried to force themselves on her, Ding held them at bay, reminding them that their futures depended on Lalu and the price she fetched.

It was also Ding who found a scrap of coarse netting to protect her from the mosquitoes, and Ding who made sure she got a portion of any food they forced from frightened woodcutters and farmers in isolated hamlets. Ding. A friend who cared about her as a person? Or an enemy looking out for his own interests, protecting her like a landlord protects his property? She had to find out.

Riding night and day, with sleep coming in

stolen snatches, Lalu lost track of time, and she worried that they would reach Shanghai before she had a chance to speak to Ding without fear of being heard. But finally, on a scorching hot afternoon, as they were ascending a narrow valley choked with sword grass, thorny bushes, and vines, Ding's horse, doubly burdened, fell behind.

Lalu waited impatiently for the distance between them and the rest of the group to widen. Then, relieved and nervous that the opportunity to talk had come at last, she blurted, "Why did you force me to come with you when I might have escaped?"

"Have there never been soldiers in your village?" Ding asked.

"Yes."

"Then you know why I did not leave you."

Lalu thought of the soldiers who had come to their village. She had been a child, too young to remember how they had behaved, but she remembered the farmers' resentful comments to her father just before the bandit raid and Ding's accusing, "You're better off with us." Were soldiers really as bad as bandits? Or, as Ding claimed, worse?

Lalu shook her head. Better or worse, the soldiers were not important. What was important was that Ding had believed he was helping her to escape from them. Would he help her escape now?

"I could have hidden from the soldiers and found

my way to a village or city," she suggested cautiously.

"A girl like yourself does not have one chance in ten thousand of traveling alone safely. But say you had made it to a village or city without being kidnapped or raped or killed, what would you have done then?" Ding asked, imitating Lalu's careful phrasing.

"I would have found work."

"Doing what?"

What kind of work could she do? No one would hire her as a farm laborer, but her fingers, used to a hoe, no longer held a needle with ease, and she had never learned to cook. What else was there? Babies. She loved caring for her brothers, and she was good with them, able to tease a smile from them when no one else could.

"A nursemaid. I could have been a nursemaid for a wealthy family."

"And before you knew what was happening, you would have found yourself with life inside you from the master or one of the men servants."

Lalu flushed. "My parents gave me better home teaching than that."

"It's not a matter of home teaching," Ding said patiently. "You would have had no more choice than I or any of the others here had a choice to become bandits. And when you were discovered with child, it would have been you who were blamed and thrown out into the street. Then what would you have done?"

Lalu ignored his question. "What do you mean you had no choice in becoming a bandit?" she asked, puzzled. "You're educated. I can tell by the way you speak. And your manners. You're cultured, refined. Different from the others. From me."

He hesitated. "I was a magistrate," he said.

Again he paused, and when he spoke at last, his voice was heavy with barely controlled anger and grief. "A sudden change in the political situation forced me to flee for my life. I sent my wife and children back to her parents for safety and joined the bandits to seek revenge."

A magistrate! Lalu twisted round to face him. "Does Chen know?"

"Of course."

"Isn't he afraid of what you might do when you go back to being a magistrate?"

Ding laughed mirthlessly. "Water once spilled cannot be gathered again."

"But what about after you've had your revenge?" Lalu persisted.

"You think I'm different from the other bandits," Ding said harshly. "I'm not. Chen. Zhuo. Zhu. We're all the same. Outlaws. And none of us will ever be anything else."

His voice softened. "Lalu, I know your mother and father did not raise you to be sold to a house of leisure, just as my parents did not raise me to be a bandit, but we have no choice except to follow the paths Heaven has allotted us."

Lalu, facing forward again, said nothing. But as they climbed up the steep trail to the ridge where Chen and the others waited, she vowed she would never accept the path Ding claimed Heaven had assigned her.

She waited until darkness fell on the sleeping camp. Then, hoping the bandits' snores and the horses' restless stomping and whinnying would smother the crunch of broken rocks beneath her feet, Lalu edged past the two scouts keeping watch. Slowly and carefully, she worked her way back to the crest of the narrow valley the horses had climbed with such difficulty only a few hours before. By the time she reached it, the moon had risen, coating the dry, dusty grasses and bushes with a pearl white sheen. She closed her eyes briefly, murmured a prayer to Guanyin, the Merciful One, and began her descent.

The trail was steeper, more treacherous than she remembered. Half walking, half crawling, she clutched the jewelry hidden in her waistband with one hand and reached out the other to steady herself. Thorns ripped her palm. Stifling a cry, she jerked back, slipped, and fell.

Sharp bits of gravel pierced Lalu's thin cotton

pants. Dust and dirt filled her mouth, nostrils, and
eyes, making her choke as she hurtled down the
sheer slope. She grabbed blindly at a bush, catching
twigs which snapped beneath her weight. Skin tore
off the sides of her hands, her legs. She felt an
ankle lodge in a rut and dug in, reaching wildly for
a nearby boulder. The effort pulled her arms half
out of their sockets, flinging her sideways, knocking
her head against a huge rock face, wedging her
right shoulder and hip in a crevice.

The blow stunned Lalu. She lay still, her
breathing ragged and shallow. Gradually, the
darkness receded and the pain of torn muscles and
bruised flesh sharpened. There was the sound of
muffled voices.

High above her, spread out around the rim of
the valley, pitch pine torches flickered like fallen
stars, signaling a search. She leaned back. Solid
rock gave way to black emptiness, and she fell
again, landing in soft, stinking mire.

She had fallen into a cave, she realized. Was it
a lair? Stories she had heard of children carried off
by tigers pulled her upright. Hands stretched out
before her, she staggered toward the moonlit crack
through which she had fallen. Fingers touched
wall. Wincing, Lalu leaned her weight against her
stinging palms, using the wall for guidance and
support as she blundered toward the sliver of light.

Small, soft bodies wriggled beneath her hand,
and she heard a curious gnashing like the grinding

of hundreds of tiny teeth. Clamping her jaws together to keep from screaming, Lalu crouched low. Her body crawled with gooseflesh and she gagged as the nauseating odor of dung mingled with the stink of fear. Ghostly wings brushed her face and neck. Spirits? Then what were the creatures clustered on the walls?

Through the fissure, moonlight beckoned, promising release from this hideous trap. Lalu dragged herself toward it. Chills racked her sweat-soaked, fiery body, impeding her progress. Then, all at once, the crack of light vanished in a rush of flapping wings, and she found herself trapped in total darkness. Sobbing uncontrollably, she sank defeated onto the muck-covered cave floor.

Just as suddenly as the splinter of light had vanished, it reappeared, with a bat silhouetted against the pale white beam. A bat, symbol of good luck. A sign from the gods? Again wings whirred past Lalu, blocking the opening. Bats. She was in a bat cave!

Relief swept over Lalu in a wash of giggles. She pictured her brothers' faces as she told them the story. How they would laugh! Except, of course, they would never hear her tell the story. "You must be quiet or I won't come back," she had told them. Did they think she had disappeared because of them? Or had her father told them that he had sold her for seed?

"The bitch has got to be around here some-where."

Lalu flinched as though she had been slapped. How could the bandits have come so close so quickly? Her eyes riveted on the only opening through which they could come, she backed crablike into the farthest recesses of the cave. Her limbs, cut, bruised, scratched, and sore from the long hours on horseback and her recent tumble, screamed protest, but she dared not stop. Trem-bling, slipping, straining, she fell onto her knees and crawled until she hit solid rock. There, huddled against the unresisting boulders, she hugged her soiled knees to her chest and whispered, "The bandits can search for days and never find me here."

Like a Buddhist nun repeating her beads, she said the same sentence over and over. At last, mesmerized by her own whisperings, her tightly clasped arms relaxed their hold, and she collapsed into exhausted slumber.

A piercing, high-pitched squeaking and the furious flapping of wings wakened Lalu. She rub-bed her eyes. While she had slept, the sliver of moonlight in the cave opening had turned into a golden beam. And then she realized the golden beam was not sunlight, but a pitch pine torch.

Unable to move, she stared as the flames moved

EIGHT

closer until the light shone above her, blinding, and she heard Ding say, "Don't you understand, you cannot escape your fate?"

NINE

The rickshaw puller stopped abruptly, throwing Chen and Lalu forward. "House of Heavenly Pleasure," he called.

Lalu climbed out onto the hot, dusty street in front of a massive wall the height of two men. She gazed up at the broken glass embedded into the wall's rim. Was it there to keep out thieves or to prevent escapes?

"Come on, come on, stop gawking like a country bumpkin," Chen said, herding Lalu toward the gatekeeper's house.

The gatekeeper's stare made Lalu as uncomfortable as the garish purple jacket, apricot pants, and thick layers of makeup which Chen had insisted she wear.

"A new pullet ready for plucking," Chen said.

The gatekeeper grinned. He opened a small side door. "The Madam will be pleased with this one."

The sight of wide green lawns dotted with rock

gardens, lotus ponds surrounded by graceful weeping willows, and a spectacular main house with carved wooden railings, vermillion columns, and green-glazed roof gave Lalu no pleasure. She knew Ding was pleased that he had persuaded Chen to bring her here, for he had told her in one last conspiritorial whisper, "I know from my days as a magistrate that this house serves only rich, famous, refined gentlemen. Do as you are told, try to please, and you are bound to be bought out soon and installed as a concubine or perhaps even a secondary wife in some wealthy household." But she had her own plan, one that depended on her sale price being kept as low as possible.

Doubling over as though from pain, Lalu felt under her jacket, seeking reassurance from the bulge of jewelry hidden in her waistband. Against the magnificence of the House of Heavenly Pleasure, it seemed abysmally insufficient to carry out her scheme.

"Hurry up," Chen said.

Lalu's hands dropped from waist to feet. "These shoes are too small."

Chen grabbed Lalu's collar and twisted.

"You're creasing my jacket," Lalu said.

He glared down at her. "Don't rub the scales under a dragon's neck," he warned, pushing her past the spirit gate. "One false move and you'll wish you had never been born."

An arrogant housemaid ushered them past

growling guard dogs into a cool, shadowy ante-room. The wood paneled walls, latticed ceiling, painted glass lanterns, and thickly carpeted floor confirmed Lalu's worst fears. Drained of hope, she allowed Chen to propel her behind a heavily carved blackwood chair.

"Now remember," Chen instructed. "When you smile, don't expose your teeth. If the Madam asks you to walk, take small, mincing steps so she won't notice your big feet. If she offers us food, don't wolf it down, take delicate little nibbles."

A middle-aged woman, tall and elegantly dres-sed, emerged from behind a double panel of em-broidered silk. "Is the girl such an ignorant peasant that she needs last minute coaching?" she asked.

"No, no, of course not," Chen said, pivoting to face her and bow.

The Madam turned to Lalu. "Come out from behind the chair so I can see you."

Encouraged by the woman's warm smile, Lalu walked out boldly.

"Small steps," Chen hissed.

"Your feet are not bound," the Madam said. "Why?"

"I was..."

Chen interrupted. "I assure you, they have been bound and can easily be bound again." Under the Madam's icy stare, his voice trailed off weakly.

"I asked the girl."

"I was needed in the fields," Lalu explained.

The Madam walked over to the round lacquer table between the two blackwood chairs. She dipped a square of cloth in a bowl of scented water. Her long tapered fingers wrung out the cloth, and she wiped Lalu's face free of rouge, dye, and rice powder while Chen hovered nervously.

"The girl looks half starved."

"We're from the North where we've been suffering famine from a bad drought," Chen said quickly. "To be very honest, the girl's parents, my brother and his wife, died from hunger. Since the wife and I took her in, we've given her what we can afford, but we're poor ourselves, which is why we're forced to sell the girl much as it grieves us."

"Spare me your fairy tales," the Madam said.

She sat down. As Chen bowed and backed onto the edge of the opposite chair, the Madam reached for the silver waterpipe on the table between them. She opened the lid of the tobacco box. Using little silver tweezers, she picked up a pinch of tobacco which she poked into the pipe. She lit the pipe, drew two leisurely puffs, emptied out the smoked tobacco, and repeated the process.

Watching her, Lalu felt a small surge of hope. She had seen her father act in this same unconcerned manner when he wanted to beat down the price of what he was buying. Pretending to smooth out her jacket, she patted the little cache. If the Madam proved a shrewd bargainer, her jewelry might be enough to buy her freedom after all.

Chen squirmed. His mouth opened and closed like a fish caught in a net gasping for air. He mopped his face with the backs of his hands, his sleeves. Finally, he burst out, "The girl may be thin, but it makes her look delicate. Like expensive porcelain."

"Our patrons are more interested in flesh and blood," the Madam said dryly.

"Oh, you'll find plenty of both. And in the right places too."

"So, she isn't a virgin."

"Oh no, I didn't mean to imply...oh, how could you think?" Chen stammered, horrified. "Of course she's a virgin. My sister-in-law was a pious woman, and the girl has been strictly brought up."

"You all say that, but where will I find you to get my money back if she is not?"

"I'll give you my address in the city."

"You just said you were from the North."

"Look, if you don't want the girl, just say so. There are plenty of Madams that will," Chen snapped.

The Madam set her pipe down. "Perhaps, but none of them can afford to pay the price I can. Isn't that why you're here?"

"I'm asking eighty thousand cash."

Aghast, Lalu cried, "You gave my father two bags of seed worth no more than a small string of cash!"

Chen leaped out of his chair and slapped Lalu.

NINE

"You're damaging your merchandise," the Madam said calmly. "And the price you're asking is absurd. Even a goddess wouldn't bring you that much."

Chen drew himself up. He tapped his puffed out chest with his index finger. "I know what you charge for one night with a virgin."

The Madam's brow wrinkled in barely concealed disgust.

"This is not the kind of house you frequent. Virgin or not, we cannot offer our guests an untutored peasant obtainable for free from their own servants' quarters. Before your 'niece' can serve as a daughter of joy, she will need time and money poured into her for lessons in singing, dancing, and all the other techniques of her new profession." She paused. "I can offer you fifteen thousand cash."

Chen stormed toward the door. "Come on. Let's go."

Lalu thought swiftly. If she went with Chen, he would probably take her to a Madam as filthy and coarse as the landlady at the inn where they had spent the previous night. The price of sale would be lower, one that her bits and pieces of jewelry would surely cover, but would she be able to trust the woman not to steal them from her?

She studied the impassive face of the Madam who sat before her. Her eyes glittered as sharply as the points of finely honed needles, yet her touch had been gentle, and she had spoken kindly. She might be hard, but she would be fair.

Chen shook Lalu. "Come on."

She hesitated.

His fingers dug into her shoulders. "Move."

"No, I won't."

"You're mine, you'll do as I say."

As though Chen and Lalu had not spoken, the Madam said, "Twenty thousand."

"Seventy thousand," Chen countered.

"Twenty-five thousand."

"Sixty thousand."

"As you said yourself, there is a famine in the North. Soon girls like this one will be sold for three or four thousand cash, perhaps even a single bag of seed," the Madam said.

"Fifty thousand."

"Thirty thousand. That's my last offer."

Chen released Lalu. "All right, but I might as well be giving her away."

The Madam reached into the strongbox beside her and counted out the strings of cash. Still grumbling, Chen snatched them and left.

As soon as the door closed behind him, Lalu unpinned the gold and silver earrings, jade bangle, and jade button from beneath her jacket. Within the rich grandeur of the anteroom, the earrings seemed tarnished and dull, the jade less green. She rubbed them against her new clothes and held them up to the Madam. "I want to buy myself."

NINE

The Madam rose. "Sit down," she said, guiding Lalu into the blackwood chair across from her.

Lalu thrust the jewelry up at the Madam. "If it's not enough, I'll work off the balance."

The Madam closed Lalu's fingers around the jade and silver and gold, gently forcing the fists onto Lalu's lap. "Keep your jewelry, it might be useful to you someday."

"If it can't buy my freedom, what use can it have?" Lalu demanded.

A twinge of pain flashed across the Madam's face. "The man who sold you called you Lalu. Is that your name?"

Lalu nodded sullenly.

"But he is not your uncle."

Lalu shook her head.

"How did this man who is not your uncle come to sell you?" the Madam asked.

Lalu uncurled her fingers. She stared at the jewelry she had believed would save her, the specks of blood where the sharp points of the earrings had pierced her palms. If the glittering baubles could not buy her freedom, perhaps her story would. Choosing her words carefully, she told how Chen had forced her from her father, her attempt to escape, her capture, and the beating she had received.

In the silence that followed, she heard someone in another part of the house plucking the strings of a lute. The slow, wailing melody fell like a rain of teardrops. Would another girl brought for sale at some future date hear her play or would the Madam let her go?

"Do you know what a cormorant is?" the Madam asked.

"It's a bird that eats fish," Lalu said, puzzled.

"Have you seen how fishermen use them to catch fish?"

"They put rings around the birds' necks so the birds can catch the fish but not swallow them. But what..."

The Madam interrupted. "Like the cormorant, I have a person I work for. You saw me pay for you, but you are not mine to do with as I choose."

Lalu fought back tears. Had she, like her father, gambled and lost? "I don't understand."

The Madam pointed her ringed fingers at the rich silk hangings, bowls of semiprecious fruits, antique vases, and carved jade and ivory bric-a-brac that filled the room. "All this is a result of my labor, yet it is not mine any more than the fish a cormorant catches is his. I work for a high government official who offers me the protection I need to live. But you are fortunate Chen brought you here today."

Lalu leaped out of her chair. "You mean you will let me buy myself back?"

"Lalu, you have great strength. Don't waste it on fighting for the impossible," the Madam said. She pointed to a scroll on the wall. "Look at that bamboo. It's strong, but it bends in the wind, just as you must learn to do."

"Then why did you say I was lucky Chen brought me here today?" Lalu cried.

"Normally, I would not be able to buy a scrawny, dark-skinned girl with feet like dragon boats, but today I have a special buyer who does not care about such things, someone who will take you to America."

PART TWO

第二部份

1872

TEN

Like the hold of the ship, the San Francisco customs shed was dimly lit, but at least the lanterns did not pitch and sway; and the air, though stale and stinking from the press of unwashed bodies, did not reek of vomit or human waste. If anything, the din from hundreds of voices, mostly male, had grown louder. But there was life and excitement in the shouting, joyful expectation in the rush for luggage, relatives, and friends.

Lalu, waiting for her turn to come before the customs officer, caught the contagion of nervous excitement, and she felt the same thrill, bright and sharp as lightning, that had shot through her when the Madam had told her she was going to America, the Gold Mountains at the other end of the Great Ocean of Peace.

"I have never been there, but Li Ma, the woman for whom I bought you, says there is gold everywhere. On the streets, in the hills, mountains, rivers, and valleys. Gold just waiting to be picked up...."

"Gold that will make me rich. So rich, no one, not even Old Man Yang, will dare speak against me if I go home," Lalu had whispered, ignoring the rest of the Madam's words.

Hugging herself inwardly, she had pictured her parents' and brothers' faces when she gave her father the gold that would make him the richest man in the village. The pride they would have in her, their qianjin. And she had held fast to this picture, as to a talisman. First, when the Madam had turned her over to Li Ma, the crotchety, foulmouthed woman who would take her to the Gold Mountains. Then, during the long voyage, when only the men's talk of gold had kept alive her dream of going home. And now, as she folded and refolded the forged papers Li Ma had given her. For the demons who ruled the Gold Mountains wished to keep their gold for themselves, and in order to gain the right to land, Lalu must successfully pretend to be the wife of a San Francisco merchant.

Over and over, during the long weeks crammed in the hold of the ship, Li Ma had forced Lalu and the other five women and girls in her charge to rehearse the stories that matched their papers, sternly warning, "Pass the examination by customs, and you will soon return to China a rich woman, the envy of all in your village. Fail, and you will find yourself in a demon jail, tortured as only the demons know how."

Could the torture be worse than the journey she had just endured? Lalu thought of the sweltering, airless heat and thirst that had strangled the words in her throat, making her stumble when she recited for Li Ma, earning her cruel pinchings and monotonous harangues. The aching loneliness that came from homesickness and Li Ma's refusal to permit the girls to talk among themselves. The bruising falls and the tearing at her innards each time the ship rocked, tossing her off the narrow shelf that served as bed, knocking her against the hard wood sides of the hull. The long, black periods of waiting for the hatch to bang open as it did twice each day, bringing a shaft of sunlight, gusts of life-giving salt air, the smell of the sea. The struggle to chew the hard, sour bread and swallow the slop lowered down as though they were pigs in a pen.

Lalu tossed her head, straightened her jacket, and smoothed her hair. That was all over. Behind her. No more than a bad dream. She was in America, the Gold Mountains. And soon, just as soon as she gathered enough gold, she would go home.

"Next."

Lalu felt herself shoved in front of the customs officer. She had never been close to a white man before and she stared amazed at the one that towered above her. His skin was chalk white, like the face of an actor painted to play a villain, only it was not smooth but covered with wiry golden hair, and when his mouth opened and closed, there were no words to make an audience shake with anger or fear, only a senseless roaring. Beside him, a Chinese man spoke.

"Your papers. Give him your papers," Li Ma hissed.

"My papers?" Lalu said in her native Northern dialect. "I've..."

She stopped, horrified. How could she have been so stupid? True, Southern speech was still strange to her, but during the long voyage, Li Ma had taught her the dialect, for the majority of Chinese immigrants on board came from the Southern province of Guongdong, and her papers claimed her as such. Now she had betrayed herself, proven her papers false. There would be no gold on the streets for her and no homecoming, only jail and torture.

Li Ma snatched the papers from Lalu. "Don't mind the girl's foolish rambling. You'll see everything's in order. Here's the certificate of departure and the slip with her husband's address here in the Great City."

Gold flashed as she passed the papers up to the Chinese man beside the demon officer. "A respected tradesman he is. Could have his pick of beauties. Why he wants this simpleton back is anyone's guess. Should have let her stay on in

China when she went back to nurse his old mother. But you know how men are. So long as the woman satisfies that muscle below their belt, they don't care about anything else."

The Chinese man laughed. He passed the papers to the customs officer. Again gold flashed. They talked between them in the foreign tongue, their eyes stripping Lalu, making her feel unclean. Finally, the demon officer stamped the papers. Smirking, he thrust them down at Lalu. Her face burning with embarrassment, she hugged the precious papers against her chest and followed Li Ma past the wooden barricade. She was safe.

"Look," Li Ma barked, pointing to the huddle of waiting women and girls. "Some of them are only ten, eleven years old. Children. Yet they showed more intelligence and good sense than you. Now you mark my words. That's the first and the last time I put out good gold to save your neck, so watch yourself, do you hear?" Cuffing Lalu's ears for emphasis, she herded her charges together and out onto the wharf.

Lalu, weak from lack of nourishing food and exercise, felt as if the boat were still pitching and rolling beneath her feet. But she walked briskly, not wanting to provoke another storm of abuse from Li Ma who was speeding past heaps of crated produce, sacks of flour and beans, and stacks of barrels. Above her, she heard the screech of seagulls, and beyond the wharf, the clip-clop of horses' hooves, the creak and rattle of wagons, voices deep and shrill. But she could see no further than Li Ma's back, for the same thick fog which had shrouded the Gold Mountains when they disembarked enveloped them, its cold dampness penetrating, leaving the salty taste of tears. Lalu swallowed her disappointment. She would see the mountains soon enough. Meanwhile, she would look for the nuggets the men said lay in the street.

Beneath the sickly glow of street lamps, she saw horse droppings, rats feasting on piles of garbage, rags, broken bottles. Metal glittered. A discarded can or gold? Stooping to grab it, Lalu did not see the rock until it stung her cheek. Startled, she looked up just as a mud ball splashed against Li Ma's back.

Li Ma whirled around. "You dead girl," she screamed at Lalu. "How dare you!"

She broke off as high-pitched squeals and cries burst from the girls around her. Through the heavy mist, Lalu made out white shadows, demon boys, hurling stones and mud, yelling, words she did not understand but she could feel.

"You dead ghosts," Li Ma cried, shaking her fist at them.

Giggling, the boys concentrated their missiles on the short square woman. Without thinking, Lalu picked up the stones that landed nearest her, flinging them back at the boys as fast as they could throw them. Years of playing with her brothers had made her aim excellent and the boys soon fled.

Li Ma fell on Lalu. "Stop that you dead foolish girl or you'll have the authorities after us."

"But they started it."

"Are you so dim-witted that you don't know you're in a demon land? The laws are made by demons to protect demons, not us. Let's just hope we can get to Chinatown before they come back with officers or we'll find ourselves rotting in a demon jail."

Shouting, pushing, and shoving, she hurried them up steep cobbled streets with foul smelling gutters, past wagons pulled by huge draft horses and unwashed demon men loafing on upturned barrels until they reached narrow streets crowded with Chinese men. Chinatown. Even then, she did not permit the women and girls to rest. But the warm familiar smells and sounds soothed Lalu's confusion, and she barely felt Li Ma's parting cuff as she herded them down a flight of stairs into a large basement room with more young women and girls like herself.

"Those with contracts come over to this side, those without go stand on the platform," an old woman in black lacquer pants and jacket directed.

Lalu held out her papers. The old woman took them. She pushed Lalu in the direction of the women without contracts.

"No, I belong over there," Lalu said, trying to take back the papers.

The old woman snorted. "What a bumpkin you are! Those papers were just to get you into the country. They have to be used again."

"But Li Ma said..."

"Don't argue girl, you're one of the lucky ones," the old woman said. She pointed to the group of women with contracts. "Their fates have been decided, it's prostitution for them, but if you play your cards right, you may still get the bridal chair."

A shocked murmur rippled through the group of women. One of them took a paper from an inner pocket. "I have a marriage contract," she said. "Not what you suggest."

"And I! And I!" the women around her echoed.

The old woman took the contract from the young woman. The paper crackled as she spread it open. "Read it!" she ordered.

The young woman's lips quivered. "I can't."

The old woman jangled the ring of keys at her waist. "Does anyone here read?"

The women looked hopefully at each other. Some shook their heads. Others were simply silent. None could read.

"Then I'll tell you what your contracts say." Without looking at any of the papers, the old woman continued, "For the sum of your passage money, you have promised the use of your bodies for prostitution."

"But the marriage broker gave my parents the passage money," the young woman persisted.

"You fool, that was a procurer, not a marriage broker!" She pointed to the thumb print at the bottom of the paper. "Is that your mark?"

Sobbing quietly, the young woman nodded.

"Well then, there's nothing more to be said, is there?"

"Yes there is," a girl said boldly. "I put my mark on one of those contracts, and I knew what it was for." Her face reddened. "I had to," she added.

"So?" the old woman, hands on hips, prompted.

"The contract specifies the number of years, five in my case, so take heart sisters, our shame will not last forever."

"What about your sick days?"

"What do you mean?" the girl asked.

"The contract states your monthly sick days will be counted against your time: two weeks for one sick day, another month for each additional sick day."

"But that means I'll never be free!"

"Exactly."

Like a stone dropped in a pond, the word started wave after wave of talk and tears.

"Keep crying like that," the old woman shouted, "and by the time your owners come to get you, your eyes will be swollen like toads."

"What difference does it make?" a voice challenged.

"Depending on your looks, you can be placed in an elegant house and dressed in silks and jewels or in a bagnio."

"Bagnio?"

"On your way here you must have seen the doors with the barred windows facing the alleys, but perhaps you did not hear the chickens inside, tapping and scratching the screens, trying to attract a man without bringing a cop. Cry, make yourself ugly, and you'll be one of those chickens, charging twenty-five cents for a look, fifty cents for a feel, and seventy-five cents for action."

Slowly the sobs became muted sniffles and whimpers as stronger women hushed the weaker. The old woman turned to Lalu's group. "Now get up on that platform like I told you."

Silently Lalu and the other women and girls obeyed. When they were all on the platform, the old woman began to speak.

"This is where you'll stand tomorrow when the men come. There'll be merchants, miners, well-to-do peddlers, brothel owners, and those who just want to look. They'll examine you for soundness and beauty. Do yourself up right, smile sweetly, and the bids will come in thick and fast from those looking for wives as well as those looking to fill a house.

"When the price is agreed on, the buyer will place the money in your hands. That will make the sale binding, but you will turn the money over to me. Do you understand?"

The women and girls nodded. A few murmured defeat.

The old woman pointed to some buckets against the wall. "There's soap and water. Wash thoroughly. You will be stripped for auction."

"Stripped?"

"Women in the Gold Mountains are scarcer than hen's teeth and even a plain or ugly girl has value. But when a man has to pay several thousand dollars for a woman, he likes to see exactly what he is buying," the old woman said.

She grabbed a tight-lipped, thin, dark girl from the back of the group. The girl stared defiant as the old woman ripped off her jacket and pointed out scars from a deep hatchet wound, puckered flesh the shape of a hot iron. "Look carefully and be warned against any thought of disobedience or escape." She threw the girl's jacket onto the floor. "It will be the bagnio for you. If you're lucky."

She pulled the women closest to her down from the platform and herded them toward the buckets of water. "Now get going, we've wasted time enough."

All around her, Lalu could hear the sounds of women and girls preparing themselves for auction, but she made no move to join them. It had taken all her concentration to make out the words that had been spoken in the strange Southern dialect, and she was only just beginning to feel their impact.

She had been duped, she realized. By the soft voiced, gentle Madam, a cormorant who had nothing to give except to its master. By Li Ma, the foulmouthed procuress charged with Lalu's delivery to the auction room. By the talk of freemen whose dreams could never be hers. For the Gold Mountains they had described was not the America she would know. This: the dingy basement room, the blank faces of women and girls stripped of hope, the splintered boards beneath her feet, the auction block. This was her America.

Through a haze as chilling as the fog that had surrounded her at the wharf, Lalu became aware of warm breath, an anxious nudging. It was the thin, dark girl the old woman had exposed as warning.

"Didn't you hear what the old woman said? You're one of the lucky ones."

"The Madam in Shanghai said that too."

"But it's true. There are women far worse off than you. Like those smuggled into the Gold Mountains hidden in padded crates labeled dishware or inside coal bunkers. Many of them don't survive the journey or arrive so bruised and broken they cannot be sold." The girl leaned closer and lowered her voice still further. "Those women are taken straight to the same 'hospitals' as slave girls who have ceased to be attractive or who have become diseased. There, alone in tiny, windowless cells, they're laid on wooden shelves to wait for death from starvation or their own hand." She brightened. "But you made the journey with papers and a woman to look out for you. You're thin, but beautiful and sound."

"What does that change except my price?"

The girl took Lalu's hands in hers, holding them tight, quieting their trembling. "You must learn as I have to let your mind take flight. Then you won't feel, and if you don't feel, nothing anyone does can hurt you."

ELEVEN

On the auction block, Lalu closed her eyes against her own nakedness and the men who milled around, poking, prodding, and pinching. Bids fell like arrows. Gold pieces, cold, hard, and heavy, dropped into her outstretched palms.

A woman's harsh voice ordered her to dress and Lalu knew she had not been purchased for a wife. She no longer cared. With the heavy lethargy of a sleepwalker, she pulled on jacket and trousers and followed the woman up the steps into the same dirty, narrow streets she had walked the day before.

As they retraced the journey to the wharf, Lalu's nose wrinkled at the stink of garbage and manure, the splatter of mud, but she made no effort to look for promised gold or dodge the stones of demon boys, the drunken leers of demon men.

Vaguely, she realized the vessel they boarded was smaller, less crowded than the one that had brought her across the Ocean of Peace, that the journey was shorter, and Portland, their destination, a sunnier, less hostile demon city. Dimly, she heard a young, handsome Chinese man greet them, felt him take her from the woman and place her on a mule.

He had a packstring of ten mules, eight loaded with supplies, one which he rode, one for Lalu, and as her mule jogged beside his, he attempted to draw her into conversation. He was Jim, he said. A packer Lalu's master, Hong King, had commissioned to fetch his slave.

He spoke kindly and in Lalu's same Northern dialect. But the fragile cocoon she had spun around herself was too warm, too comforting to break with talk, and she did not respond.

Nine days' travel through thickly wooded trails brought them to Lewiston, a strange town made up of tents, makeshift houses of canvas stretched across wood frames, and buildings so new Lalu could smell the rawness of the wood.

"All mining camps look the same," Jim said, guiding the packstring through rutted dirt streets crowded with freighters and horsemen shouting and cracking their whips. "There's a main street, dusty in summer, muddy or snow covered in winter. A few saloons. A dance hall. Two or three stores. A jumble of wooden shacks and tents where everything has to be kept in tins for protection from mice and rats. And Warrens, the mining camp where you will live, is just like that." His arm made a sweeping movement. "Like this. Only smaller."

Languidly, Lalu's eyes followed the sweep of Jim's hand. Hogs rooted in piles of empty tins, potato peelings, old hambones, eggshells, and cabbage leaves. Chickens, pecking and clucking, strutted on and off the boardwalks and around broken pots, shovels, worn-out kettles, boots, and other rubbish, breaking up clouds of flies that covered clumps of stinking manure. A rat burrowed in the spilled-out entrails of a dead dog. From the buildings and tents lining the street came music, raucous laughter, bursts of gunfire, and breaking glass.

"Those are saloons," Jim said. "Wine shops. Like your master's. Only his is empty of customers. That's why he bought you.

"There are sixteen hundred men in Warrens, twelve hundred Chinese, four hundred or so whites. And there are eleven women. Three are wives, two are widows, and a half dozen are hurdy gurdy girls. But they're all white. You'll be the only Chinese woman, an attraction that will bring men, Chinese and white, from miles around."

Like scalding water, Jim's words unraveled the casing of Lalu's cocoon, and she found herself floundering. She halted her mule. From the hitching rack edging the boardwalk, between horses patiently waiting for their masters, she could clearly see the demons inside the saloons. Some simply smoked and drank or competed at squirting streams of brown tobacco juice. Others crowded around gaming tables or hopped and bounded like performing monkeys, their arms around short-skirted, painted demon women whose heeled boots pounded rhythms on crude plank floors.

Did her master expect her to dress like these half-naked, painted demon women? To dance with hairy, unwashed demon men? To lie with them, one woman among sixteen hundred men?

"If you don't feel, nothing can hurt you." She repeated the thin, dark girl's words, reminding. But then she saw again the hurt in the girl's defiant black eyes, the puckered flesh, scars real and deep.

Abruptly, Lalu kicked her mule and urged it forward, galloping past the string of mules and Jim, out of town, and across the meadow, splashing across shallow streams, snapping off low hanging branches in groves of cottonwoods edging the banks, frightening unsuspecting red squirrels, birds, a deer. Finally, the mule staggered, wheezing, blowing, and hollow eyed, its sweat-caked flanks dripping foam. Ashamed, Lalu slowed to a walk.

When the mule's breathing evened, she stopped. Dropping her reins over the pommel so it could drink from the creek, she looked back across the blue green sea of meadow grass and camas. There was no sign of the packstring, not even a faint tinkling of the lead mule's bells. She glanced up at the fiery sun. It would be dark before the pack mules, each one loaded down with five hundred pounds of freight, covered the same length of ground her mule had galloped, and Jim would never dare risk leaving them to pursue her. She could ride on alone, away from the future that waited for her in her master's saloon.

Where would she go? To return to Lewiston or Portland or San Francisco would mean capture, possible mutilation, the bagnio, or perhaps even the "hospital." Yet she could not stay out here on the open prairie or in the mountains skirted and crowned with pines. She had no food and no means to obtain it. And she had no protection against the barbarian demons who made their villages in the open spaces beyond the filthy mining camps.

Dirty and black haired, they wore strange combinations of feathers, beaded skins, and demon shirts and pants, and they lived in tents that looked like funnels turned upside down. Their voices, when they demanded liquor and trinkets, were insolent, their manners arrogant. Yet they seemed sad, their black eyes as mournful as those of the homeless refugees she had once seen pass through her village. But they were frightening too. Armed with bows and arrows, small, sharply honed hatchets, and sometimes rifles, they threatened violent death, and when any approached, she could sense angry fear in the white demons she had run from.

The woman who had taken Lalu to Portland had said the white demons were merely overgrown children, unable to control their selfish desires and passions. But Lalu knew they could not be dismissed so lightly. Armed with guns and knives, they were as quick to fight and shoot as the bandits who had snatched her from her village. Only these "bandits" had the power to make laws, laws that made people like Li Ma afraid when Lalu had thrown stones back at the demon children who had attacked them.

And there was that first day on the trail with Jim, when he had stopped to read a trail marker carved on the smoothed-out trunk of a cottonwood. The characters had warned of robberies by demons and Jim had led the packstring deep into the woods until he found another, safer trail. As they traveled, his eyes searched out more markers warning of assaults, a lynching. "Out here, there is no law," he had said. "Every man is his own court and his revolver is judge and executioner, especially executioner."

Later, he had pointed out China herders, demons who jumped claims for Chinese miners and guarded them while they worked. But to Lalu, the China herders had looked the same as the other demons: tall, brawny, hairy, and dirty. Like the demons in the saloons in Lewiston. The ones in the saloon where she would be forced to work.

She groaned. If only she could gather up

enough gold, she could go home. But the gold she had expected to find lying everywhere was buried in hard rock or in beds of ice cold mountain streams. She would need pick, shovel, and pan. Her hand dropped to her waist. The jewelry hidden in her waistband might buy the needed outfit and, with luck, she might even find a gulch that had not already been worked clean. But without protection, she would never live to take home the gold she found.

Ding was right. She could not escape her fate. Slowly, she wound her reins around the pommel of the saddle and dismounted so the mule could graze while she waited for Jim.

By the time Jim reached the creek, the cold crescent moon had risen high in a sky bright with stars. Lalu, huddled beneath saddle blanket and bedroll, watched him unload the mules, picket two, and turn the others loose to graze.

From a distance, with his queue coiled beneath the bulge of his Stetson, his red flannel shirt, and corduroy pants stuffed into high leather boots, he could be mistaken for a demon. He even wore guns in his belt and chewed tobacco like they did. And he used a demon name. Yet he had treated her as kindly as he would a younger sister. Until today, when he had talked of Warrens, the saloon where she would work. Then his voice had been cold and hard, deliberately cruel.

He lit the pine knots Lalu had gathered from a distant grove and prepared a simple meal of rice and salt fish. They ate, the silence punctuated only by the click of their chopsticks, an occasional whinnying, the crackle of pitch oozing out of pine knots.

When Jim scooped the last grains of rice from his bowl, he built up the fire until it blazed like a bonfire in the cold night air. Lalu set her bowl, still more than half full, onto the grass and held her hands up to the flames, but they could not warm the chill inside her, and she shuddered.

"Lalu, I know the saloons gave you a bad shock. That what I said and the way I said it was brutal. But when you see a demon, you must confront it. Only then will the demon disappear."

Lalu stared into the red orange flames. "Will the demons in the saloons disappear?"

"Most of the men in the saloons are prospectors or miners, decent men who spend weeks, sometimes months alone in the hills or gulches and canyons, so when they come into camp, they sometimes act crazy. But they don't mean any harm. They're just celebrating or trying to drown their disappointments and fears in drink and gambling."

"Drink, gambling, and me," she said, fighting back angry tears.

Jim cut a fresh quid of tobacco. For a while there was only the sound of chewing, a lone coyote's howl which burst into fitful yaps so rapid the wild bark surrounded the camp. Then, the chaw of tobacco firmly lodged in his cheek, he said, "Eleven years ago, when I came to America, all I had was my strength. So I sold it to a company that contracted labor. At that time a healthy Chinese man marketed for four to six hundred dollars, one with extraordinary ability a thousand. It took me six angry, bitter years to work off my debt, but now I am my own man. And you will be your own woman again, I promise you."

TWELVE

Day after day, as the packstring toiled up the steep mountain trail, Jim told Lalu more about the Gold Mountains and demon customs and drilled her in the English words she would need for her work in Hong King's saloon. But at night, after they had eaten, Jim would build up the fire, cut himself a fresh quid of tobacco, and they would talk about themselves.

Lalu spoke of home, her sale to the bandits, her dream of riches, the auction block. And Jim told of his father's death when he was not much more than a boy, his confusion and fear as each day his mother's touch grew colder and lighter, her eyes more vacant until one day she did not move at all. He had run away then, he said. But her eyes, dark hollows in a face bleached white as mourning, pursued him. So he returned, only to find her dead, buried without her son to mourn her, and he had run again, this time to the Gold Mountains.

Long after the fire had died down, when there

was only the soft crumbling of logs into ash, the tinkle of a mule's bell, Lalu would lie wide awake, savoring the shared closeness of their talk, promise of a deeper intimacy. A promise all the more precious as each night the moon grew larger, the distance separating her from her master shorter.

Resentment swelled in her at the thought of Hong King. She had not been sold to pay for her father's mistake, why should she now pay for the mistake of a stranger? A greedy old man who had scorned the miserable, ill-paying jobs permitted Chinese for the gamble of a demon saloon.

"He's old, he will not misuse you, his last hope," Jim had said. But she had heard the concern in his voice and she knew he was not sure. Nevertheless, she understood honor demanded Jim deliver her to Hong King. He was a packer. She was his freight.

In the darkness, listening to Jim's soft, steady breathing, she thought of his promise that she would be free. He intended to buy her. Of that she was sure. But Hong King had paid twenty-five hundred dollars in gold for her, more than the cost of Jim's entire packstring. Was that why Jim was teaching her vocabulary for use in a saloon, drilling her with an almost frightening urgency? Because he could not pay for her now? And why, when he talked of everything else, was he silent on this?

The questions tore at Lalu, surfacing each time she woke from thin, fitful slumber. But when

TWELVE

Warrens' unpainted shacks came into view after twelve days' hard travel, she was as empty of answers as she had been the afternoon she had urged her mule into the futile gallop across the prairie.

"These first cabins are the Chinatown," Jim said, bringing the packstring to a halt. He pointed across the creek to a huddle of irregular, steep-roofed shanties set down in a clearing surrounded by mountain and forest. "That's the white section of Warrens. Hong King's saloon is the first one on the left-hand side of the main street. You can't miss it."

Lalu's eyes widened in panic. "You aren't coming with me?"

"It wouldn't look right if I brought my string into camp when the stores I deliver to are here."

"But I'm part of your goods."

Jim's face, strong as newly carved rock, darkened as though shadowed by a cloud. "You know you're more than that."

"Then ride in with me now."

"I'm a packer," he reminded. "In camp for two, three days, gone for three weeks, a month. If you're to survive, you must stand alone."

So he couldn't buy her. At least not yet.

Disappointment and fear stuck like fishbones in her throat. "Tonight, in the saloon..."

"I'll be there."

Lalu pulled short her reins, dropped them.

Swift as a bird's wing, Jim's hand reached out. Their eyes locked.

"Remember," he said, his voice husky. "You have a friend in me. Always."

Not trusting her own voice, Lalu nodded. She pressed her knees against the mule. It trotted forward obediently, its hooves drumming across the wooden bridge, the sound a hollow echo in the painful emptiness of her heart.

Dust rose from the garbage-strewn, unpaved main street, but it did not hide Lalu from the knots of demons idling on the raised boardwalks, and they crowded round her, jerking the mule to a halt.

A demon lifted Lalu off the mule and set her on the ground. "Here's Polly," he said.

Remembering Jim's admonition that there was nothing demon men admired so much as pluck in a woman, Lalu fought down a rising panic and drew herself up straight. "Lalu. Me Lalu."

The men laughed. "The China doll talks." One of them pushed open the swinging doors behind him. "Hey, Charlie," he called. "Here's Polly."

A demon, bearded like the others but shorter and hatless, emerged, squinting in the sudden glare of light.

"Lalu." She pointed to herself. "My name Lalu."

From behind, bony hands seized her, and Lalu found herself looking into a Chinese face as cracked and creased as parchment. The fleeting moment of relief as she took in skullcap and silk robe, the dress of a gentleman, vanished when the man spoke.

"A slave does not choose her own name," he snapped in Chinese. "From now on you are Polly. Is that understood?"

Lalu knew this man must be Hong King, that she should lower her eyes and bow assent, yet she could not. His grip hardened, the long nails digging through the thin fabric of her jacket and into her flesh.

"Yes, I understand," she said.

Twirling the hairs sprouting from the wart on his chin, Hong King turned to the crowd that had gathered. His thin, white lips spread in a satisfied smile, exposing black stumps of teeth and sour breath. "You want look see, you come Hong King's saloon tonight," he said.

He turned back to Lalu. "The first taste will be mine."

In the pale afternoon sunlight that filtered through the filthy upper window of Hong King's shack, Hong King looked more than old. He looked dead. His skin, stretched taut over fragile bones, was the color and texture of old wax, and his mouth gaped wide, drooling spittle onto Lalu whom he clasped tightly, his long, brown stained nails scraping her flesh raw.

He blamed Lalu for his lack of arousal. Her feet were so big and her hands so coarse he thought he was in bed with a man. And her ignorance was not to be believed. Did he have to tell her everything?

Finally, his loins stirred weakly and he mounted her. And in the stain of blood that proved his victory, Lalu saw the death of yet another dream.

THIRTEEN

That night, in the narrow room behind Hong King's saloon, the hurdy gurdy girl Hong King had paid to dress Lalu applied the last of the makeup. She stood back and admired her handiwork.

"Good. Now hair," she said.

She crimped Lalu's hair in the front, parting it in the middle and drawing it back behind the ears, making the ends into finger puffs on top of the head, then indicated Lalu should remove her jacket, the restrictive bodice underneath.

Lalu hesitated, thinking of the day her mother had told her she must wear the bodice to flatten her breasts or be called a wanton. What would her mother say if she knew her daughter had been forced to submit to an old man's feeble, humiliating rutting?

She closed her eyes, trying to shut out the memory of Hong King's demands, his naked, withered flanks, and shriveled manhood, picturing Jim instead. His skin, a pale ivory above the line of his

Stetson, a dark golden beneath. The gleam of his
teeth when he laughed. The ripple of his muscles
when he lifted heavy packs. All warmly familiar.
All lost to her now.

The hurdy gurdy girl tugged at the bodice. "I
help?"

"No," Lalu said. "I do."

The corset which replaced her Chinese bodice
squeezed the breath out of Lalu, and the whalebone
stays cut into her flesh. Did demon women's bodies
naturally curve like the necks of vases or did the
lacing of the corset work like footbinding cloths,
changing the shape of the body after years of
suffering, Lalu wondered.

She looked at the tightly corseted girl with
renewed interest.

The girl smiled. "Small pretty. Good for catch
husband."

Jim had told Lalu that the hurdy gurdy girls in
Warrens were recruited from Germany, that they
owed the price of their passage to an agent, and
that they paid it off by working at the saloon,
dancing, encouraging the customers to buy more
drinks. But often, a miner wanting a wife would
pay off the balance due, making her free to marry.
Was this girl trying to tell Lalu that tiny waists, like
bound feet, were necessary for a good marriage?
That marriage was still possible despite Hong King?

The girl smoothed Lalu's red silk skirt. "My
dress too long for you. I make short."

THIRTEEN

"No." Lalu opened the back door, letting in the sweet scent of pines. "You go. I do."

The girl drew a derringer from inside her bodice. She nodded toward the door that led to the saloon. From the other side came the sounds of stamping feet, table thumping, shouts for Polly. "You need."

Lalu gaped at the tiny gun. Jim had said the hurdy gurdy girls were not required to give favors. He had not told her that they had to carry guns to ensure it.

"I get," Lalu assured the girl.

She closed the door and leaned against it. She had hoped this narrow room with just enough space for a small potbelly stove, chair, bed, and commode would be hers alone, for Hong King lived in a cabin in the Chinatown. Now she wondered if he expected her to entertain in it. A fist pounded on the opposite door, the one that opened into the saloon. She could not delay her entrance much longer.

In three steps Lalu crossed the width of the room and picked up the high-heeled boots the girl had left. Like the dress, they were too long. She wadded rags into the toes, slipped them on, and clumsily hooked together the long rows of tiny buttons.

She stood, took a step, teetered precariously, and fell. Leaning heavily on the commode, she pulled herself upright. A painted, frizzy-haired stranger with bare shoulders frowned at her from the mirror above the commode. Lalu stared. She was Hong King's slave, his to use as was his right, but she had not yet become a whore.

Dropping back down onto the chair, she unhooked the high-heeled boots and slipped on her soft cloth shoes. She took out pitcher and washbowl from the commode and scrubbed her face clean of rouge, powder, and paint. She recombed her hair, smoothing out the silly finger puffs. Finally, she wrapped a lace shawl around her naked shoulders.

She looked at her image in the mirror. The sad-eyed woman she saw was not the girl her family had known, but the face was clean and honest. With a toss of her head, she strode to the door, twisted the knob, and plunged into the saloon.

"Hey Polly, where you been keeping yourself?" a high-pitched voice piped above the indistinguishable roar.

Tanned arms swept her off the floor. "Been waiting for me, huh, kimono girl?"

Stronger arms in red flannel snatched her away. "No, me. I'll make her queen of the bull pen."

Lalu forced herself to smile at the demon holding her. "Put me down. I working girl," she said, using the words Jim had taught her.

"So what're we waiting for?" he slurred, burying his beard in her neck.

Lalu did not understand the words he used, but she could feel their meaning, the scratch of his beard. She pushed the demon's head away. "You wrong idea. I waiter girl. Nothing more."

"Sure," he said, swinging Lalu on top of the bar. "And here's to the darlingest, sweetest fairybelle that Warrens ever saw."

As he lifted his glass in a toast, she sprang free and dropped behind the bar. She crouched low, listening to the rapid pounding of her heart, the catcalls, shouts, finger snapping.

Hong King set down the scales he used for measuring the pinches of gold dust miners used to pay for their drinks.

"I didn't pay twenty-five hundred dollars plus freight just for you to hide," he snapped.

Ripping off her shawl, he yanked Lalu to her feet. Immediately she felt herself swung back on top of the bar. Through a gray haze of cigar smoke, she looked down at the men crowded into the saloon. Bearded demon miners in faded flannel shirts and worn corduroy pants stuffed into heavy, mudcaked boots. Smooth-faced Chinese in traditional blue cotton jackets and pants or full-sleeved, long-tailed Chinese shirts hanging out over coarse demon trousers. Gamblers and speculators gaudily dressed in satin coats and colorful vests with gold watch chains hanging across well-padded bellies. Adolescents suddenly become men bursting out of ready-made suits too tight and short. They were all the same. Hungry. Like the coyotes she heard howling in the night. And she was their prey.

"Why she's pretty as a heart flush!"

"A little doll, no taller than a broom."

"Give us a dance, doll!"

Lalu stood paralyzed.

"Hey booze boss, make her dance," a demon shouted.

Hong King tapped the counter. "The men told you to dance."

Didn't he realize she couldn't? That her deformed feet would not let her dance?

A demon pulled out a harmonica. "Name your tune."

In the crowd of upturned faces, Lalu saw Jim's. Relief washed over her. And then embarrassment. How could she meet his gaze?

Eyes downcast, she lifted her hem and pointed to her feet. "No good. No can dance."

"Look at those chinee feet!" the demon directly in front of Lalu marveled.

He grabbed a foot and snatched off her shoe. A second demon seized her other foot and another lifted her off the bar. Pressed close to the demons, the stink of sweaty underwear and liquored breath overpowered the less offensive smells of sour tap drippings and smoking coal oil lamps.

"Put me down," Lalu said, kicking.

"She got her spunk up!" the demon holding her laughed. He tossed her in the air.

"Wild as a mustang," the demon who caught her agreed.

THIRTEEN

She drummed her fists against his chest, but it only made him squeeze her tighter. She squirmed, straining to see over his shoulder. Where was Jim? She knew her refusal to meet his gaze had betrayed her shame. But he had said he was her friend. Always. Then why wasn't he helping her?

Suddenly, as she was being tossed to another demon, Lalu realized he was gone. All the Chinese had vanished. Except Hong King. And he was red with fury. At her, not the demons, she was sure.

She was alone. Just as she had been this afternoon when she rode into camp. Just as she had been since Chen took her from her home. Frantically, she searched for the word Jim had said she might need. What was it? Move? With the men tearing at her, she could not think. Run? Go? No, git! That was it!

"Git," she cried. "Git up and dust!" But the demons only laughed harder.

"Put the girl down."

Narrow chested and round shouldered, the demon who had spoken was shorter and far less brawny than the one holding Lalu, but as he walked toward them, his gun drawn, a path opened for him, and Lalu felt the grip on her loosen. She slid to the floor.

"No need to pull your iron Charlie, we just joshin' her."

Charlie's eyes, blue as camas, flashed. Startled, Lalu recognized the shaggy red brown hair and beard, the skin more pale than the sunburned leathery faces surrounding her. He was the demon who had been called to come out and gawk at her when she arrived, the one whose eyes had flashed when Hong King shouted at her.

"You've had enough funning for one night," Charlie said.

"She's the Chinaman's girl and he don't mind."

Angry voices murmured agreement. Hong King scowled. Charlie tossed a buckskin bag of gold dust onto the bar.

"Step up and liquor at my expense," he invited.

During the rush to the bar, Charlie whisked Lalu back into her room behind the saloon. Jim was there waiting.

"Are you all right?" he asked anxiously.

"Yes, but I don't understand."

Jim smiled. "This is my friend, Charlie Bemis. He owns the saloon next door."

"I've got to get back to the saloon," Charlie said. "But you tell Polly to holler any time those fools get too liquored up and start getting rough and I'll be right over." Flashing Lalu a smile, he slipped out the back.

Jim translated. Then he explained how when he had seen her in trouble, he had gone to fetch Charlie. "No one dares mess with him, he can keep a tin can dancing in the air with his six-shooter and everyone knows it."

"So can you."

Jim pointed to his belt. It was free of holster and pistols. "It isn't wise for me to wear my guns in camp."

"Not wise? Everyone out there had a gun! Or two. At least the demons did. Even the hurdy gurdy girl Hong King paid to dress me had a gun. And she told me to get one."

"Lalu," Jim interrupted. "If I had tried to help you, I couldn't have just walked in like Charlie did and say, 'Put her down,' I would have had to shoot to kill, and you can be sure I'd be strung up on a tree by now, with a half dozen Chinese beside me."

"But you said the Chinese in this camp outnumber the demons."

"The white men have the power."

"How can you call them men when they act like demons?" Lalu exploded.

"Would you call Hong King who used you like a whore a man and the man who saved you tonight a demon?" Jim retorted.

Lalu's eyes stung with tears. "How could I stop him?"

His voice softened. "Lalu, you did, and you will continue to do what you must in order to live. There's no shame in that. But Charlie is a good man. Trust him, he'll be a true friend to you."

FOURTEEN

Lalu's life fell into a strictly circumscribed routine revolving between the saloon and Hong King's shack. Though she slept in her own room behind the saloon, Hong King refused her permission to talk to anyone except customers from whom he could profit and Charlie and Jim whom he did not dare refuse. But in the five months since she had ridden into Warrens, Jim had returned only four times, a total of twelve days. She lived for those days.

And her day of freedom.

Each night, after the saloon emptied, she carefully swept up the dirt clotted with tobacco juice, cigar butts, ashes, and spittle from the rough planked floor. Then, in her own room at the back of the saloon, she panned the sweepings for the gold dust the men dropped when they dipped into their pokes to pay for their drinks and gambling. Occasionally, like today, there was a nugget.

Using her hairpin as a tweezer, Lalu picked it up

and added it to her cache. She ran her fingers through the little pile of clean gulch gold. In the glow of the coal oil lamp, the cold flakes glittered like stardust and the nuggets jingled merrily as they hit the jade button and bangle at the bottom of the leather pouch. It had taken Jim six years to buy his freedom. Would it take her as long?

"Lalu."

She knew the person knocking was Jim, only he called her that anymore, but she could afford to take no risks. Quickly, she hid her poke in the chamber pot and shut the door of the commode before she called, "Come in."

Frosty October wind and fallen leaves gusted into the room with Jim. He hung his hat on the nail behind the door and stamped his feet, blowing into his cupped fists. Lalu pushed the wooden box of floor sweepings and pan of water from the floor in front of the stove.

Jim stoked the fire. "Mining?" he asked with a chuckle.

Lalu laughed. "White men mine the rich claims. Chinese mine the ones that have been worked over, Hong King mines the miners, and I mine Hong King."

Jim laughed with her. "A few years ago, in Virginia City, a man bought a saloon and burned it down. Then he hired two men with a rocker to work his claim while he stood guard with a shotgun. At the end of ten days he'd reclaimed ten thousand dollars in dust that had spilled through the cracks in the floor."

"I'd like to burn this place down," Lalu said, setting the chair in front of the stove for Jim.

He sat down and cut a fresh quid of tobacco. "Be careful. If Hong King finds out you're cheating him, there's no telling what he'll do."

"Every time that old fraud takes a pinch of dust for a drink, he makes sure some gets wedged beneath his long nails!" Lalu blazed. "But don't worry, Charlie says the number of customers has quadrupled since I came, and there's so much more dust in the sweepings I'm sure Hong King doesn't realize I'm taking some for myself."

Jim worked the lump of tobacco in his cheek. "You're planning to save enough to buy your freedom and then go home, is that it?"

Lalu sat down on the bed. The ticking, stuffed with hay, rustled, making sounds like dry, anxious sighs. From the day she had run from the saloons until this moment, Jim had never again mentioned her freedom, and since her delivery to Hong King, the unkept promise had lain like a stillborn child between them. Why was he bringing it up now? How should she answer?

"When my father came back from Mongolia," she said at last, "he made my brother and I learn the saying — The copper corner of one's hometown is more precious than the gold or silver corner at the end of the earth."

Jim spat. The wad hit the red-hot side of the stove, making it sizzle. "Did he also teach you— The moon is not always round, flowers do not always bloom, and men do not always have a happy reunion?"

"No, he didn't."

"Lalu, you think of your family as they were when you left them, but by the time you've saved enough to go back, your brothers will be grown men, your mother and father, grandparents."

Lalu picked at the quilt covering the bed. "So?"

Jim leaned forward. "When we were on the trail, I heard you call in your sleep for your father, and I've seen your face when you sneak out to hold Mrs. Saux's baby. It's not Melina you're crooning nursery rhymes to, it's your baby brother. And when you look at the sky and sniff the air and feel the wind, you're halfway round the world again, in your father's fields. Your family means everything to you. But you're dead to them."

Lalu jumped to her feet. "That's not true."

"Then why haven't they responded to the letters you asked me to have written for you?"

"It's only been five moons."

"That's time enough for a reply," Jim persisted.

"The letters might have been lost. Or maybe they're dead, or they've become landless refugees."

The excuses she had rehearsed over and over to herself tumbled out in desperate denial.

Jim walked over to Lalu and gripped her

shoulders, forcing her to look him in the face. "Your father sold you."

"He had no choice," she defended.

He shook her, his voice hard and cold as the hoarfrost coating the ground outside. "Face it! You're dead to them," he repeated.

"No," she cried. "I'm their qianjin."

He released her. "If you still believe that, you're as much a slave to your own falsehoods as you are to Hong King."

For a long time, neither one of them moved or spoke. Finally, Jim reached for his hat. "I just came to say goodbye. It'll start snowing soon and Warrens will be snowbound. I won't pack in again until the trail clears. Maybe May or June."

"So long?" Lalu said, her lips quivering.

"With all my trips, I'm hardly here anyway," Jim said. "Charlie will look out for you."

"He watches over me like a China herder. If there's any trouble, I just run out the door and wait in his back room until he straightens it out." She paused. "But we can't talk. Not like you and I do."

"That way you can't argue."

For a moment, Lalu felt an urge to break through the veneer of their argument to the real feelings and issues running like deep currents beneath. Feelings and issues she could not label but which she sensed were far different from those their words expressed. But when she took Jim's hat and hung it back on the nail, she simply said, "Don't let's part with bitter words between us."

She poured tea from the pot on top of the stove and handed the cup to Jim. "I know you're right. No letter is going to come."

Small dishes of food, spirit money, smoldering incense, and freshly turned earth marked Jim's grave. Lalu knelt and knocked her head on the ground.

Three days ago he had been alive. Then his mule had stumbled on French Creek hill near Secesh Creek. She pictured the worn trail they had traveled together. The steep ascent. The broken ridges, dark ravines, and densely wooded gulches. The bleached out bones of horses in purple canyons, the remains of those who fell. And she remembered the way her heart had lodged like a lump in her throat as the mules' steel shoes clinked against the rocky ledges where a single misstep meant certain death. Still, she could not believe Jim's broken body lay rotting beneath the damp earth and decaying leaves on which she knelt. He was too experienced a horseman. Too careful. Too alive to become mere memory.

She thought of their last night together, the dark sadness she had seen in his eyes. Had his mother's eyes looked like that? Had hers when she had retreated from a reality she could not bear? The angry words they had hidden behind haunted her. Had she unwittingly helped weave his shroud?

Footsteps crunched on gravel. "When do you suppose Jim will come back to eat all that food?"

Lalu jerked up angrily. Charlie, a spray of faded, windblown columbine in one hand and fiddle in the other, loomed over her.

"When Jim come smell flowers?" she snapped.

Charlie laid the scarlet blooms beside the dishes of food. He leaned against a fallen tamarack and clinched his smooth brown fiddle between shoulder and bearded chin. "If Jim can eat and drink and smell, do you suppose he can hear too?"

"Of all my tunes, I think he liked this one best. Said it reminded him of the river near his village."

The tune Charlie played was not mournful, but as the high, clear notes danced through the air, Lalu felt the tears she had struggled to hold back trickle down her cheeks. She wiped them off impatiently. But like a dam finally, suddenly burst, the tears became a steady stream.

Without a word, Charlie laid down his fiddle and took Lalu in his arms. She leaned against him, shaking, her body racked with huge sobs as she wept.

For Jim.

And for Lalu.

Both dead forever in a strange land.

PART THREE

第三部份

1875

FIFTEEN

In the chill of predawn darkness, all Warrens slept. But inside Hong King's saloon, the coal oil lamps blazed and Polly, her face and dress damp with perspiration, searched for something else she could clean or wash or scrub.

The bottles, cigar vases, and glasses on the shelves behind the bar glittered, and the bar itself, polished until it was slick enough for skating, glistened darkly. The towels customers used to wipe foam from mustaches and beards hung, pressed and folded, from the edge of the counter, and Polly could see her own distorted image in the shiny brass rail around the bar's base. Beside the windows on the side and front of the saloon, the four gaming tables sat squarely, the chairs tucked beneath green felt coverings brushed up like new. The stove, freshly reblacked, gleamed in the center of the room, and the deep wooden boxes the men spat in were filled with fresh sawdust.

The odor of whiskey and stale tobacco lingered,

clinging like an indelible brand to the walls and Polly's clothes and skin. But there was nothing left to clean. To keep her from facing the black man's words.

"You ain't no slave, honey," he had said. "They is no slaves in America, not fo' ten years."

The words should have filled her with joy. Instead, she felt a sense of betrayal as strong and deep and painful as when her father had picked up the bags of seed. For if the black man was right and she was not really a slave, why hadn't Charlie told her?

Her limbs, overcharged with energy a moment before, felt weak, and she jerked out a chair, upsetting the piles of chips stacked at the center of the table. Automatically, Polly restacked them, then sank limply onto the chair.

She could understand why no Chinese had spoken. Those loyal to Hong King would not, and the others either did not know or did not dare to speak. And the white men and women had no reason to interfere. But Charlie? He was always reading books and newspapers so he had to know the law. In fact, he was often asked by miners to solve minor disputes, for his knowledge and reputation for honesty made his judgments respected even when disliked. Yet he had remained silent on this. Why?

She had trusted him, given herself to him, at first because he was kind and gentle and she was lonely and afraid, and then because she believed he cared. But he had betrayed her.

The door swung open, and Charlie walked toward her, his footsteps loud and unnatural in the quiet. "When you didn't come, I thought you'd gone down to Chinatown. Then I saw the lights and got worried."

She looked up at him, her eyes dark bruises of pain. "Why you not tell me I not slave, that I not belong Hong King?"

The hesitation before Charlie spoke was fractional but Polly, her senses scraped raw, felt it.

"Who said you're not?"

"Black man come to saloon tonight. He tell me his people come from Africa. Like me, stolen from village and bring here, but man name Lincoln make war and they free. He free, I free," she said, her English deteriorating under the strain.

"The Civil War was fought to free Negroes."

"You mean law for China people not the same?"

Charlie pulled out a chair. "It's more complicated than that."

He took out his tobacco pouch and pipe, stuffed the bowl, tamped it down, lit it, and took a deep drag. The smoke drifted between them.

"Years ago, special laws were passed in California to forbid the kind of auctions and contracts that made you a slave, but the laws only raised the price of slave girls."

"How law make black man free and raise price for me?" Polly demanded.

"Because girls started running away and it cost their masters a great deal of money to get them back."

She shook her head. "I not understand."

"I don't understand it myself," Charlie sighed. He puffed thoughtfully.

"The system works something like this," he said at last. "If you ran away from Hong King, he would trump up some charge that would force the sheriff to come after you. Then, when you were caught, Hong King would get a friend of his to bail you out, and once he got you back, he would drop the charges."

"You tell judge Hong King make me slave."

"I wish it were that simple, but judges and lawyers are not always indifferent to bribes, and there's a problem with language and translators, and technicalities in the law. There are the highbinders from the tongs as well. They've been known to kill those who've tried to escape and those who've helped them too."

The words Charlie used were long and he spoke quickly, but Polly understood only too well what he was saying. Striving for control, she balled her hands into tight fists beneath the green felt table covering. "So you not tell judge."

Charlie walked over to the stove. He finished his pipe, knocked the ashes onto the grate, and sat down again. "I will if you ask me. But you should know that the majority of women who have braved the courts have lost, and of the few that have won, most have been deported. Do you want to take that chance?"

"What 'deported' mean?"

"Sent back to China."

Polly's fists tightened, her nails dug into her palms. What would happen to her if she were sent back to China? Though she had told Jim she knew no letter would come, each New Year, under the pretext of illness, she had gone to Li Dick, the herbalist, and given him money to send home for her. Three New Years had come and gone without reply, and she could no longer avoid the truth. Either her mother and father were dead, or she was dead to them. Either way, she could not go home.

But the gold she had saved would buy some land. Land she could farm like her father had taught her. If the villagers permitted. She thought of the widows' struggles in her own village. The suspicion and hostility a single woman would arouse. And she knew if she went back to China, she would have to marry.

All through her childhood she had believed what her mother had told her, that getting married and birthing children were a woman's happiness. Even after she had begun working in the fields and doubts had seeped in like dust from a summer storm, she had not really questioned the truth of what her mother had said. Wasn't marriage for a woman as inevitable as birth and death? That was why, when Chen had bought her, she had tried to offer herself to him, to be his wife, thinking that would make everything all right. And during the journey into Warrens she had hoped and even prayed that Jim would buy her for his wife. Now she was not sure. Her mother had said a woman belongs to the father of her sons. If she married, wouldn't she be exchanging one master for another?

She looked up at Charlie, saw his lips move.

"The Negroes had terrible lives," she heard him say. "They came to America in chains and were forced to work under conditions you can't begin to imagine. Many of them barely had enough to eat. They were at the mercy of their masters and overseers. Whipped. Raped. Sold at will. Things aren't so bad for you here.

He lifted a corner of her silk skirt, rubbed it between his fingers meaningfully, pointed to the snow white petticoats beneath. "You have beautiful clothes and plenty to eat. I keep the men in line and Hong King..." He paused.

"You're better off than a lot of free people," he finished abruptly.

Polly stared at the man who sat before her. Was this the man she had allowed herself to love? This man who did not seem to care that he had to share her with another. This man who dared look her in the eye and say she should be content with her lot.

She turned from him and walked to the window. For more than two years now, they had shared the same bed. But what did he know of her life beyond his bed and cabin and Hong King's saloon? She had never told him about the long weeks crammed into the hold of the ship, scarcely able to breathe the stale, stinking air. The humiliation of standing naked on an auction block. The way her gorge rose each time Hong King mounted her. Her fears that if she did not obey she would be sold to a bagnio or sent to a "hospital." She had not told him because she had thought he could understand without words. She had been wrong.

Polly laid her forehead against the cold pane of glass. Outside a meadowlark sang, its haunting melody reminding her of the three robins she had saved after Mr. Grostein's cat had killed the birds' mother.

At first, they were content to fly around her room, but soon they began pecking at the window, demanding to be let out. So Charlie built a cage for them, and she hung the cage on a tree outside. But their cries tore at her, and finally she opened the door, letting them fly where they pleased. Then one day Mr. Benson, the butcher, came to the saloon and handed her a cigar box with three stiff bodies crusted with blood.

He was sorry, he said. He knew how much the

birds meant to her, and he had reprimanded his clerk severely. But the way they hovered, demanding scraps, had been annoying, and if she had kept them in the cage Charlie had made for them, his clerk would not have killed them.

Charlie had told her the same thing, and she had tried to explain why, even though she mourned the birds' deaths, she did not regret leaving them uncaged. But he had not understood. Then how could she make him understand her own need to escape the cage that held her?

Slowly, Polly turned and walked back to the table. "Charlie, your father doctor, and you have fine education and beautiful home in Connecticut. But you run away because your father try make you surgeon and you not want. You work as deck hand on ship, and when you reach San Francisco, you hear about gold rush, and you try mining. Now you saloon keeper and gambler. But if you want change again tomorrow, nothing stop you. You free.

"I only daughter of farmer who cannot read or write. But I too want be free."

Charlie took Polly's hands in both his own. "Do you think I want anything less for you?" he asked sadly. "But it just doesn't seem possible."

She pulled away. "Maybe not now, but I will be free. Now, please leave. I must lock up."

Charlie started walking toward the door, then wheeled about sharply. "Polly, I know you're skimming off gold from Hong King, that you're saving it so you can buy your freedom like Jim did, but it won't work."

"You need not worry," she said coldly. "I not ask you to help."

He ran his fingers through his beard, tearing at it. "Listen to me. Jim tried to buy you. Not once, but three times. At first, Hong King said Jim could have you for ten thousand dollars, four times what he had paid for you. But at the end of the summer when Jim went to him with the money he had borrowed and saved, Hong King laughed in his face. So Jim came to me and borrowed three thousand more. Still he refused. Then Jim asked me to try. That's when Hong King said he would never sell you, not at any price."

Too late, she understood the dark sadness in Jim's eyes, the reason for the angry words. And yet she could not believe it. "Why Jim not tell me? Why you not tell me?"

"Jim made me swear I wouldn't. He said hope was all you had to live for, and he couldn't rob you of that."

SIXTEEN

They talked until dawn, but it changed nothing. Jim was still dead, the gold Polly had labored so hard to save simply so much dust.

As they walked back to Charlie's cabin, Polly pieced together bits and pieces of conversation she had overheard about Hong King. He had come to the Gold Mountains more than twenty years ago when gold was more plentiful, the laws against Chinese less severe, and it had taken only seven years for him to mine enough to go home a rich man. But on his way back to San Francisco to buy his passage, he was persuaded to join a game of fan-tan, and he had lost everything. Twice more he had saved enough for a comfortable retirement, and twice more he had gambled it away, the last time on renting the saloon in Warrens and buying her.

His gamble had paid off. She had made him rich, more than rich enough to retire. Yet he never talked of going home. And why should he? Home meant a wife as old as himself, household responsibilities, a siege of requests for help from poor relatives. Warrens meant gold, an enviable life of self-indulgence. So long as he had his slave.

She should have seen that long ago. But she had not wanted to. Wasn't that why she had not confronted Jim during their last night together? That night he had accused, "You're as much a slave to your own falsehoods as you are to Hong King." And she had been. All through her years in Warrens. How else could she have endured Hong King's sour breath and clawing hands, his blind rages when he lost at gambling, his pleasure when he caused her pain. But now there could be no more turning away from the truth.

She would never be free. Not until Hong King was dead.

With that realization, Polly became silent. Then, while Charlie slept, she slid out of bed, dressed, and took his Winchester off its rack.

She had never learned to shoot. Jim would not teach her, and she had never asked Charlie. But she had gone with Charlie on hunts, and she knew from the trampled brush and grass, small sunken rocks, and bushes stripped of leaves and berries, that the trail she was following had been made by bears. Large rocks overturned in search of insects, a dead tree trunk clawed wide open in play, and long streaks of plowed up ground where cubs had romped confirmed her suspicions. Then, in the distance, she saw a brown she-bear streaking along, her cub not far behind.

She did not follow them. Neither did she attempt to shoot the deer stealing silent and ghostlike through the brush. Nor the wild goats, some as big as ponies. For this, her first attempt to shoot, she had decided on a fool hen, a bird too stupid to fly from danger.

She knew the birds' brownish gray feathers blended so skillfully with the texture and color of bark that they were almost impossible to spot. But she also knew that the cock liked to beat its wings against its breast and that the noise would betray its location. She stopped to listen.

Squirrels, mere flashes of red against moss green trunks, chattered as they ran from tree to tree. Bees from a nearby hive hummed as they competed with yellow butterflies for the little blossoms that flowered between the gnarled roots of giant pines. But there was no sound of wings beating against breast.

Wishing more sunlight penetrated the hoary weave of firs, larches, cedars, and pines, Polly searched the branches methodically, the closest ones first, then farther and farther. Nothing. Disappointed, she turned to go, then froze. There, on a branch not thirty feet from where she stood, a fool hen's gray brown tail feathers drooped over pine needles.

Pulse quickening, Polly lifted the rifle and pushed ten long, soft nosed shells into its magazine. She sighted her target and fired.

The explosion split her head into a thousand brittle fragments of pain. The smell of burned powder, bitter and acrid, filled her nostrils. She lowered the rifle. Squirrels scolded alarm. Wings flapped as birds, sounding shrill warnings, made good their escapes. But the fool hen sat on the same branch. Unaware of danger, it blinked stupidly, as though annoyed by the sudden noise.

Its tiny beadlike eyes made Polly think of Hong King and his refusal to let her go. Abruptly, she lifted Charlie's rifle. Just as abruptly, she lowered it, swallowing, her mouth suddenly dry. Hong King was not a bird, but a man. An old man who would surely die before many years passed, leaving her free, without blood on her hands.

Insects hummed, distracting, and she thought of the dragonflies her brothers used to catch and tie with thread then force to fly from one boy to the next. After a while, their gossamer wings would fall off but, captives still, they could not stop. So they crawled from one master to the other until, exhausted, they died.

Polly's hold on the rifle tightened. Hong King was not just any old man. He was her master. And if she wanted her freedom, she would have to kill.

For the third time, she lifted the rifle. She blinked, willing the myriad of red dots that clouded her eyes to disappear. Concentrate. She must concentrate. And steady herself.

She breathed deeply. The soft, damp, loamy smell of the wild filled Polly's nostrils. She sighted the bird and fired.

Again she felt the rifle recoil, the explosion shatter the peace. Heart pounding as savagely as her head, she forced herself to look at the branch, the bird she had aimed for. Empty.

For a moment, she thought the bird had flown. And then she saw it. Caught in a bush where it had dropped. Dead.

And Hong King would be next.

SEVENTEEN

Polly hid the rifle under her bed. She wished she had a smaller, less obtrusive gun like the hurdy gurdy girl's derringer or Charlie's pistol, but she would not be able to get one without attracting attention and the key to her success would be surprise.

As she washed and changed, Polly planned her strategy. It should not be difficult, for like the fool hen, Hong King had grown complacent, leaving her to run the saloon while he played fan-tan or poker. If she waited until he came to pick up the night's earnings, she could shoot him without witnesses, and he would be dead before he realized that behind his slave's placid mask lay a woman scheming for freedom. Fixing a bright smile across her face, Polly opened the door to the saloon.

It was crowded, but strangely silent. Except for a tremulous, pulsating murmuring. Had Charlie discovered his rifle missing? Had he guessed her intention to shoot Hong King and come to give warning? No, he would never give her away. Not after all they had said and shared only that morning. Then what? Grimly maintaining her fixed smile, she jostled through the press of bodies.

From the way the men surged near the windows, she thought perhaps the attraction was in the street, but when she finally squeezed her way through to where she could see, she realized they were jammed around the gaming tables. One gaming table. The gaming table where Hong King and Charlie sat hunched over cards.

The lamp above the table flickered, then flashed suddenly bright, and she saw that Hong King's skin, usually dry and cold as a snake's, gleamed with perspiration as he spread his cards on the table.

"Two pair," he said.

Charlie exposed his last card. "Three aces."

The men packed around them breathed a collective sigh of release. "That a way, Charlie." "Go to it." "Show the chink!" they shouted as Charlie scooped up the pokes of gold dust from the middle of the table, adding them to the extraordinary pile already in front of him.

Dismayed, Polly watched Charlie gather the cards and shuffle for another hand. Her plan required Hong King to stay out of the saloon until closing and then to come in feeling amiable and self-satisfied, not agitated over heavy losses. Somehow she must signal Charlie to stop.

"Drinks," she called, her voice unnaturally high

and shrill. "Tangleleg, beer, champagne, brandy, forty-rod! You call, I get."

"Here's two sacks on Bemis."

"Put my bet on Hong King."

"Don't be crazy chink. Poker's an American game."

"Put mine on the Chinaman too."

"Yeah, Hong King's shrewd."

"But Charlie's the best."

"His luck can't hold much longer."

Charlie slapped the deck down. "Cut."

The men quieted. From within the wide sleeve of his dark blue robe, Hong King reached out his long, bony hand. His nails scraped across the green felt cloth, straightening the cards into a neat stack, then cut the deck precisely. Charlie licked his thumb and dealt. One card each, face down. One card each, face up.

As Hong King and Charlie tipped the edges of the hidden cards, the men pushed closer, their breath hot and damp against Polly's neck and shoulders. Anxious as they were for a glimpse, she craned forward. But already Hong King was tossing a poke from his pile of three, Charlie matching it and flicking two more cards off the deck.

Hong King's hooded eyes barely flickered as he studied the cards: his three and ace of hearts, Charlie's two of diamonds and four of clubs. But Polly knew from the way his fingers were stroking the hairs sprouting from the mole on his chin that he was well pleased by the ace, the turn in his luck.

He pushed another poke into the pot. Again, Charlie matched it and dealt: a five of spades for Hong King, a four of hearts for himself, making one pair.

All eyes turned to Charlie. He tapped the deck lightly on the tabletop, set it down, and pondered his cards, his fingers drumming silently on the mound of gold he had already won. The battered piano from Al Ripson's saloon tinkled and someone sang in a drunken quaver. The flumes by the river moaned. A lamp gurgled.

A film of perspiration covered Polly's body and she felt alternate waves of fire and ice. It was just another game, she told herself. One with only a small pot. But the tense silence, the piercing concentration on heated faces swollen ugly with anticipation insisted otherwise.

She looked at the single bag of gold in front of Hong King, then raised her eyes to look at him. Once again his fingers were entwined in the hairs from his mole, but they were tugging, not stroking. Was that one poke all he had left?

"Pass," Charlie said.

Hong King's hand dropped to the table. With the edge of his nails, he lined up his cards. "Pass," he agreed.

Sighs of relief and disappointment rippled through the crowd like shudders. Charlie reached for the deck, slid off the last cards for the hand: four of diamonds for Hong King, two of spades for himself, making two pair.

A burst of last minute betting ruptured the quiet.

"Two more on Charlie."

"Are you crazy? He's only got two pairs. The Chinaman's got a straight."

"You're guessing. Charlie's got two pair I can see."

"No guess. The Chinaman's got a two in the hole I tell you."

As Charlie threw a poke into the center of the table, talk vanished. But when Hong King pushed his last poke across the table, Polly heard a renewed stirring.

Her eyes darted from one player to the other. If Charlie's pair could win the game, why was Hong King pushing his last poke across the table into the pot? Could he possibly have a straight? Then why was Charlie tossing in three buckskin bags, matching Hong King's bet and raising him two? Was he testing, checking to see if Hong King was bluffing?

Nails pierced Polly's flesh, twisting her wrist. "I told you to bring me today's take."

Though his voice was even, cool almost, Polly could feel Hong King's anger seething beneath the surface. And all at once she understood. Hong King really did have a straight. A straight that

could win back what he had lost. A straight he
would forfeit if he did not match Charlie bet for bet.

A path opened for her and she fetched the
strongbox from behind the bar. Hong King un-
locked it and pried open the lid. With a fury he
could no longer conceal, he weighed the contents,
hurled them into the pot.

"You covered and raised one," he said, the
words spewing out in a sour, frustrated hiss.

Two pokes thudded down, scattering loose
dust. "I see you, and raise you one," Charlie said.

Hong King scraped back his chair and a ripple
ran through the crowd. Was he throwing in his
hand? Slowly, deliberately, he loosened three side
buttons, withdrew a piece of paper from an inner
pocket, and spread it on the table. The paper
crackled in the quiet. "I bet lease for saloon."

Charlie leaned back in his chair. "I already have
a saloon."

Hong King's lips tightened. His tongue darted
out, licking dryly. "I give you paper cover half my
take for next six months."

"I'd be a fool to risk gold for paper, and you
know it," Charlie said quietly.

Again Hong King's lips tightened.

"I have nothing else," he said at last.

Charlie nodded casually toward Polly. "Stake
the girl."

Polly bit her lips, choking off a cry, but Hong

King's eyes gleamed bright as the dust he was fighting to win.

"How much you stake me for her?"

Charlie hesitated. "Everything on the table."

The men around them gasped, but Polly, burning with the same anger and shame she had felt on the auction block, barely heard them.

"Final bet?" Hong King asked.

Charlie pushed all the gold into the center of the table. "Yes."

Hong King's lips twitched into a broad, toothless grin. "Agreed."

Swiftly he flipped his final card: two of hearts, a straight; then stood, knocking over his chair in his eagerness to scoop up his winnings.

Without a word, Charlie turned over his hidden card: two of clubs, a full house. He had won.

EIGHTEEN

For Polly, Charlie's cabin with its glowing stove and two chairs pulled close, the dresser made of packing crates, and the bed they shared had always been a refuge. Now, as Charlie lit a lamp and the room flared into light, she saw it as simply another shack.

Charlie wrapped his arms around Polly. His belt buckle dug into her, and she felt a wave of disgust as his body quivered with the same drunken exhilaration she had detected in Hong King after a big win. But she did not move. Even if he were not her new master, she could not stop him. He was too big. Too strong.

"Hey, you're supposed to be happy," he said, taking Polly's face in both his hands and kissing her full on the lips.

She flinched.

"Okay, so I don't rate a hallelujah chorus, but what about a simple thank-you?" he said.

A thank-you? For what? For humiliating her?

EIGHTEEN

For forcing her to break her promise that when she left Hong King it would be as a free woman. Or for teaching her that a slave had no right to make promises, especially to herself.

He took the pins out of Polly's bun. Her hair rippled down her back, a sheet of black silk.

"Tonight I ruined a man for you."

"Not for me. For the game. Because you gambler."

"It was the only way to free you."

"That what you believe. Just like Jim believe I better off if I not know Hong King not sell me. Maybe Jim right. Or maybe you right. But this my life. Not Jim life. Not yours. Mine."

Charlie strode over to the dresser and poured himself a drink, downing it in a single swallow. "All right. What would you have done?"

"I shoot him," she said, knowing even as she heard the words out loud that she could never have done it, knowing that was not the point, the reason for her anger.

"There are more ways to kill a man than with a gun," Charlie said, setting his glass down. "Hong King's lost so much face, he'll have to leave camp. For you, for us, he's the same as a dead man."

Polly slumped onto the bed. Again he had not understood, had not seen beyond her words. "You could have lost," she said tiredly.

"I didn't."

"And when you play again?"

Charlie lifted Polly off the bed and hugged her to him. She felt the worn flannel of his shirt against her face, soft as a caress.

"I would never stake you," he said, his voice surprised and hurt.

She kept her back taut. "I your slave. You can do anything."

He stood back, holding her at arm's length. "I didn't win you from Hong King so you could be my slave. You're free."

She looked down at his arms.

He dropped his hold, but the marks from his grip remained, deep red purple like the bruises from Jim when he had shaken her, demanding she face a reality neither one of them was able to confront. Rubbing the tender new bruises, she thought regretfully of the rich promise her first days with Jim had held, a promise unrealized in part because of circumstances, but more because, for all their talk, they had kept too much hidden from each other, from themselves. Was she to suffer the same loss again? And for the same reason?

In front of her, she could see Charlie, shoulders slumped, his head tossing back as he downed yet another drink. And in the mirror above the dresser, she could see his hands clasping bottle and glass. But she could not see his face, for he had lowered the mirror long ago to a height appropriate for her. Suddenly, all around her, Polly noticed similar instances of Charlie's thoughtful concern,

the curtains nailed up to shield her from prying
eyes, the second chair made smaller, the shelves
and hooks lowered, and she found herself wondering if he had indeed forced the final bet to win her
freedom and not the game.

Tonight, and the night before, she had been hurt
by his apparent betrayals, angry because he could
not understand her. But did she understand him?
From the day she had ridden into Warrens, he had
protected her, and she had accepted his help without question, as though it were her due. Now, for
the first time, she asked herself why he had come to
her rescue in the saloon. Had he interceded out of
some strange sense of Western chilvary? Or pity?
Or because he was Jim's friend. And after Jim's
death, had he continued to protect her out of loyalty
to Jim, or because he had come to care for her, or
simply to keep her in his bed?

She did not even know how or why he and Jim
had become friends. Like a frog at the bottom of a
well, she had seen nothing beyond the small circle of
blue sky that meant freedom, concentrating all her
thoughts, all her energies toward piling up the gold
she needed to reach it, never once considering it
might be gained another way. And now she could
lose that freedom which Charlie had put within her
grasp, and with it, Charlie.

Searching for words that would clear away the
misunderstandings, she began haltingly. "Charlie,
sometimes I angry with you and you with me. But

I know anger is only because you and I not understand, not believe the same way. Please, try understand this." She paused, waiting for acknowledgment.

He did not speak, but she saw his hands on bottle and glass freeze, breaking the steady drinking. Taking heart, she continued, "All my life I belong someone. My father, the bandits, Hong King. And I promise myself when I free of Hong King, I belong no man, only myself.

"You know I have gold I save to buy myself from Hong King. I want use that to build a house, start my own business. A boarding house like Mrs. Schultz."

Charlie poured another drink, gulped it. "You can't."

"You worry I not know how to cook? I watch Mrs. Schultz and I learn plenty quick."

"It's not that," he mumbled.

"Then what?" Polly demanded. "Because you think I not wife like Mrs. Schultz, not respectable, people say it bawdy house? You see, I show them they wrong."

Charlie turned to face her. "A Chinaman can't own land," he said, so softly she could barely hear him.

"But you say America have land for everyone. That people from all over the world come for the land. Rich. Poor. All the same. Anyone can have land. You said."

"Any American. You're from China."

She opened her mouth to shout denial, but the pain in Charlie's face told Polly his words had cost him too dearly to be negated by mere anger, and she sank silent onto the bed. She must think carefully, make sense out of Charlie's contradictions, her own confusion.

She knew the Chinese in Warrens did not own the stores and laundries where they worked, but she had thought that was because they planned to return to China as soon as they made enough money. Weren't the ones who came to Hong King's saloon always complaining about the loneliness of lives without wives and children, the brutish manners of white men, unfair taxes, and harsh laws? And didn't they always end their grumbling with talk of home, their eagerness to return to families left behind? But she had no family, no one to go home to.

Of course. That was it. Charlie didn't realize that she intended to remain in America. She would become an American and buy the land for her house. Land that would keep her free and independent always.

She leaped up, ran to Charlie, and crooked her arm through his. "You not understand. I never go back to China. I become American."

He pulled away. His fists clenched and unclenched. He took his pipe out of his pocket, rotated it in his hands, studying it, then tossed it onto the bed, and reached for the bottle.

Polly grabbed his arm. "What is it? What wrong?"

"The only way a Chinaman can become an American is to be born here."

She laughed. A short, bitter laugh. Here or in China, slave or free, it was the same. She needed a protector. She rubbed her hands across Charlie's back, unknotting the tight muscles. He turned. Mechanically she began unbuttoning his shirt.

He took her hands in his, holding them still. "Polly, I meant what I said. You're free. Let me be your China herder and build a house for you. You can do whatever you want to in it, invite anyone, refuse anyone. It's yours, I promise you." He smiled weakly. "You don't even have to have me."

"I..."

His fingers brushed her lips, gently silencing. "And yes, you can pay for it too."

She laughed, a joyous peal clear as ringing bells. Hearing it, Charlie's smile grew stronger, deepening into laughter that became one with Polly's. And suddenly, within the circle of their laughter, she felt finally, wonderfully free.

PART FOUR

第四部份

1890-1894

NINETEEN

Rockets whistled past the window, exploding in
showers of lemon yellow sparks against the cloudless July sky. A string of firecrackers burst, then
another, and a smell of burned powder drifted
through the open window, mingling with the fragrance of baking and cooking. From the main
street came the sounds of last minute hammering,
the gathering of men, women, and children from
outlying ranches and mines come to celebrate.

In her tiny bedroom adjacent to the larger one
in which her boarders bunked, Polly hurriedly
stitched the final gold button onto her tight-fitting
basque. Charlie had taught her to goldsmith, and
she often hammered out trinkets for sale in Mr.
Grostein's store, but these buttons made out of
five-dollar gold pieces were made for her by
Charlie.

In the fifteen years since he had won her
freedom from Hong King, the barriers of mis-
understanding which had been torn down that night

had never again come between them, for they spoke openly of everything to each other. Neither had Charlie once wavered from the promise he had made, building her this boarding house beside his cabin and giving her the protection she needed while respecting her independence. And so, to Polly, these gold buttons which Charlie had made were special, tangible evidence of his love and understanding and she changed them from dress to dress.

Downstairs, the kitchen door slammed. She bit off the thread and dressed swiftly, her fingers managing the hooks, laces, and buttons with practiced ease. Then, giving waist and skirt one last tug, she grabbed her hat off the top of the bed and ran down the stairs into the combination sitting-dining room.

Of the four rooms in the house, this was her favorite. The windows, filled with plants and flowers, sparkled behind white curtains trimmed with crocheted lace. The wood planks beneath the bright hooked rug were oiled smooth, and the room was made cozy with cross-stitched pillows and runners, and crocheted antimacassars, all of her own making. She walked past the round oak table covered with shiny white oilcloth and peered into the mirror beside the kitchen door to adjust the angle of her hat.

The face she saw was not much different from the one that had gazed out at her that first night in the room behind Hong King's saloon. The youthful freshness was gone. But the planes of skin beneath the high cheekbones were still firm and golden, and the eyes had lost their fear, the mouth its anxious quivering. Yet beneath the sparkling humor and warmth which now graced eyes and mouth was an intensity not immediately apparent, shadows of the past, the pull of unacknowledged tension.

Hat straight, Polly turned, saw Charlie stooped over the stove, licking his fingers appreciatively. She rapped her knuckles on the doorjamb. "Food is for the dance later, no snitching. Also, I promise Frank and some other boys who dance through the night that they can come for breakfast."

Charlie, fiddle and bow in hand, strode into the room. "You have enough food for a dozen dances and breakfasts, and the other women will be bringing more," he said, throwing himself onto a chair.

Wrinkling his nose, he shook his fiddle at the dirt-caked shirts in Polly's sewing basket beside the chair and said, "If you must take in laundry from miners, why on earth do you insist on doing the patching while they're still dirty?"

"Because when I get them clean and iron, I don't have to muss them."

"That's crazy."

"More crazy than you changing your saloon, where no lady is allowed, into a 'dance hall' where everyone can come, just by hanging up a canvas curtain to cover the bar and turning the pictures to face the walls?" she retorted.

Laughing, Charlie opened the door. "Come on, I can hear the fellows tuning up."

"Hey Charlie, the parade's starting without you," called Three-Fingered Smith.

Squinting against the glare of the afternoon sun, Polly could see a cluster of women in white already marching down the opposite end of the main street. "You better hurry," she told Charlie.

Nodding, he dashed across town, his boots scuffing up small puffs of dust. Polly, joining the crowd already gathered, sensed the same excitement she had once felt celebrating New Year. Of course, she was wearing white and navy blue instead of red, the breeze blew dust instead of snow, and there was no lucky New Year cake. But the festive air filled with the happy crackle of exploding fireworks, laughter, and talk was the same.

The band marched past. There were five: Charlie and Rube Bessey on fiddles, Brown at the accordion, Jenkins on the banjo, and Peter Beemer playing the flute and conducting. Polly found her feet tapping time to the music.

George Dyer, the blacksmith, clapped admiringly. "That Charlie sure can make his fiddle talk."

"Can't wait for the dance tonight," Benson agreed.

Mary Dawson nudged Polly. "You don't know how lucky you are your poor feet don't allow you to dance. After each one of these all night marathons, I walk for a month like a horse with stringhalt."

Polly laughed. "That is because all the men want a chance to dance with a lady and ladies are so few." She felt a tug on her skirt and looked down.

It was Katy, Mary Dawson's five-year old. "I can't see," Katy complained.

Polly lifted the girl. "You sit on your daddy's shoulders," she said, passing her up to her father.

Katy bounced happily. "Look at the flags!" she shouted.

Behind the huge star-spangled banner held aloft by freshly scrubbed prospectors and miners, dragon flags fluttered above two hundred Chinese marching to the crash of cymbals, gongs, and stringed instruments. Watching their proud, clean-shaven faces and handsome black queues swinging below their waists, Polly felt a rush of nostalgia for her village, the processions which ended at the temple where soul tablets marking generations gave an aura of permanence and security.

The Chinatown in Warrens was as large as her home village, and the sounds and smells were the same. There was even a small temple. But without any women or children, the men drifted in and out, always hoping that the next camp, the next job would be able to satisfy the false promises that had brought them to the Gold Mountains, and the Chinatown they created was an echo of their loneliness and disappointment, a hollow imitation of the villages they had left behind.

"It won't last," a voice said in Chinese.

Startled, Polly looked away from the twisting, swirling dragon to see Li Dick, the herbalist, deep in conversation with A Sam, the laundryman people called Mayor of Warrens.

"What do you mean?" A Sam asked.

"There's trouble ahead."

Polly looked at the smiling, cheering crowds lining the sun-washed street, the weathered buildings gaily festooned with red, white, and blue bunting, the creaking wagon beds made into colorful floats. What kind of trouble was Li Dick talking about?

"The Chinese coming in from the coast say the demons are trying to pressure the government into kicking us out," he continued.

"They tried that in '86 and we're still here," A Sam said.

"Those of us who weren't burned out, beaten, or killed."

"None of that happened in Warrens."

"No," Li Dick admitted. "But people and places change."

Despite the hot rays of sun beating down on her, Polly shivered, remembering Charlie's worried frown when he had read about the formation of Anti-Chinese Associations that vowed to force all Chinese to leave the Territory, her own agitation when news came of boycotts against Chinese merchants, laundries and stores in Chinatowns blown up, entire populations of Chinese marched out of towns at gunpoint.

Through all of it, there had been no real violence against the Chinese in Warrens, and now the troublemakers had turned their fury against a group of white people called Mormons. But she could not forget the resentful talk against the Chinese that had spilled out of the camp's saloons. Could that resentment be simmering, waiting for an opportunity to explode?

Long strings of firecrackers burst in a series of ear-splitting explosions, signaling the end of the parade, and Polly found herself pushed away from A Sam and Li Dick in the press of the crowd headed for Warrens Meadow. But the uneasiness their words had evoked remained.

She looked for Charlie, but the men and women surrounding her were too tall, and she saw only stiffly starched shirtfronts, the backs of dark suit jackets graying with dust, frilly laces, ribbons, the bobbing heads of small children. There was a determined squirming: Katy, climbing off her father's shoulders, wriggling to the ground and Polly's side.

"Are you going to come watch me race?" she demanded, wrapping her sticky fingers around Polly's.

Looking down at the candy-smeared face flushed with excitement, Polly smiled, welcoming a return of holiday spirit. "Of course. And you must help me cheer for Charlie in the horse race. Then we will go see the drilling contest, and after that you can help me get ready for the dance."

While the men and women jammed into Charlie's "dance hall" raised dust pounding schottishes, quadrilles, polkas, mazurkas, and waltzes, Polly laid out the midnight supper on the counter. With each dance, the air grew warmer, steamier, more redolent of sweaty bodies than perfume. Scarcely able to breathe, she left the platters of meat, bread, cakes, and pies, and worked her way through the crush of swirling skirts, stamping boots, and clicking heels to the window.

She pushed up the sash. Fresh air drifted in, and with it, the clink of bottles, the scratch of matches lighting cigars or pipes, for neither smoking nor drinking were permitted in the "dance hall."

She turned, waved to Charlie, nodded at friends dancing past. There was Pony Smead, the justice of the peace. Miss Benedict, the young, good-looking school teacher all the eligible young bachelors were sparking. Three-Fingered Smith who had accidentally blown off his own finger and thumb. John Long, her former boarder, whose handsome face with kindly gray eyes and neat, well-trimmed mustache towered above his wife's. Through the crook of his elbow, Polly caught Bertha's impish wink, and she laughed, glad of the dance that had brought Bertha to Warrens.

Long before they met, Polly and John had heard about Bertha's pretty brown hair, light blue eyes, and fun-loving ways from her proud older brother who boarded with Polly whenever he was in Warrens. Yet it was quite by accident that John and Bertha became acquainted. He had stopped in Florence on his way back to Ireland to see his mother. Bertha was there with her father who had traveled from Grangeville to trade his farm-cured ham and bacon for gold dust. There was a dance. The two met. Three months later they were married, and last spring John had brought his bride to set up housekeeping at a cabin near the Little Giant Mine where he worked.

Though separated in age by seventeen years, Polly had felt an immediate, special kinship with Bertha, and they visited daily, with Bertha making the mile journey into Warrens in winter on skis.

The set ended and Mary Dawson spun to a stop beside Polly. She sank onto the bench pushed against the wall. "First the parade, then the races, the drilling contest, tug-of-war, and now this," she gasped. "If you hadn't taken Katy off my hands so I could rest up, I don't know how I'd make it."

Her baby, swaddled in shawls and tucked out of

harm's way beneath the bench, whimpered. "Oh
no, not now," she groaned.

Polly swooped down and picked up the baby.
"You rest, I take care of Henry," she said. The baby,
burbling bubbles, grasped one of Polly's shiny gold
buttons and smiled.

"You're a lifesaver!"

"That's what old Mr. McGuiness tells me,"
Bertha giggled. "Swears the medicine Polly gave
him for his rheumatism makes him feel twenty
years younger."

Polly laughed with her. "You know he just like
the whiskey in it."

"Get your partners," Rube Bessey called.

Bertha and John swept back onto the floor. The
music started and a nervous young man approached.

"Oh no," Mary groaned again. "I can never turn
down the ones just out of diapers."

Polly, bouncing the baby in time to the music,
chuckled as the pimple-faced boy dragged Mary
onto the floor. Eyes riveted to his feet, his arms
pumped up and down like bellows, and Polly could
see him counting steps under his breath. Snatches
of talk drifted through the window.

"Looks like the district's about mined out."

"Said that years ago when we voted to let the
Chinamen in."

"And now most of the money in circulation is
theirs."

The words brought back Li Dick's somber

warning, her own fears of a simmering resentment, and suddenly Polly realized that in this brightly lit room alive with music, laughter, and goodwill, there were no Chinese except herself.

No matter how often it happened, the realization caught her off guard, leaving her feeling cut adrift, acutely alone. She hugged the sleeping baby to her, hungry for his warmth, his innocent trust. But the baby, not hers, only underscored her loneliness.

Leaning down, she tucked him back under the bench and slipped outside.

As Polly climbed the hill to her special place beneath the grove of pines that surrounded the cemetery, the men's words and Li Dick's warning became less real, but she knew from experience that the feeling of loneliness would take longer to subdue.

Since her freedom from Hong King, she had determined never again to suffer the ignorance in which he had kept her. She had become knowledgeable of Western foods, customs, and laws, a part of the community, counting the dancers, the men on the porch outside the "dance hall" as friends. Yet she was a stranger to them. Just as she was to Li Dick and the men of Warrens'

Chinatown who could not forgive her past, her choice of Charlie for a mate.

A twig snapped, and she shrank back into the shadows. Hidden behind a bush, she listened to boots tearing through brush, the rasp of labored breathing.

"Polly, wait up. It's me, Charlie."

She stepped out into the open. The same kind of wordless communication that had brought Charlie out of the dance to find Polly flashed between them, and they climbed silently. When they reached the top, they turned and looked down at Warrens.

Directly below and to the left, cabin windows glowed honey yellow, splashes of color flitted across the squares of light, and music blared from Charlie's "dance hall" as the camp celebrated. But to the right, in the Chinatown beyond the musical murmuring of Warrens' Creek, no band played, and the only sounds were the ordinary ones of heavy irons banging on clean clothes, the rattle and scraping of beans for fan-tan.

A thrush on a nearby branch began its night song. The soft, low notes rose higher and higher until they became a strong, beautiful melody. And then, without warning, the song ended, leaving a sad, ringing trill that accentuated Polly's loneliness, a loneliness Charlie's caring presence could ease but not entirely vanquish.

"I remember one time a man bring a performing monkey to my village," Polly said. "The man divide the audience in two and give each side one end of a rope to hold. Then the monkey walk carefully back and forth between the two sides. At each end, he stop a little bit, but he cannot stay, and so he walk again until he so tired, he fall."

She pointed down to Warrens, so clearly divided into two camps. "Sometimes I feel like that monkey."

TWENTY

A cloud of pungent steam burst from the kettle
of herb tea as Polly lifted the lid and sniffed
professionally. Just right. She replaced the lid,
eased the kettle into a basket padded thickly with
straw and newspapers, and bustled around her tiny
kitchen assembling the rest of the things she would
need for her patient, Mary Dawson's girl, Katy.
Coconut candy. Porcelain spoon. Doll.

Bertha took the doll and spoon, wrapped them in
an old washed out salt sack, and passed the bundle
back to Polly who placed it in a nest of straw above
the kettle.

"After you finish at Mary Dawson's, would you
come over to my house and help me pick up the
stitches I dropped in the sweater I'm knitting for
John?" Bertha asked.

"Sure," Polly said, clamping down the basket
and opening the door.

"Good. Then you can show me how to cook my

rice properly. John says it still doesn't taste like yours."

Polly smiled at Bertha, so slender, frail, and anxious to please. "I think it's time we play a trick on John. I will come make the rice for your supper tonight, but you don't tell him. Then we see what he has to say."

Laughing, they set off at a leisurely pace, enjoying the September sunshine, the comfortable silence of good friends.

As they neared the Dawson cabin, Bertha pointed to the teams of Chinese miners working the flatter spaces of Warrens Meadow, their picks and shovels clanging on bedrock, the gravel rattling in sluices beside neatly stacked tailings.

"I wish John worked above ground like they do," she said.

Polly thought of the one time she had gone down into a mine, the feeling of being buried, the sound of dripping water, the smell of burned powder and bad air, the rats. "He make more money," she comforted. "And he is a foreman, not have a dirty job like the muckers."

"He says miners, whether they're foremen or muckers, die young and quick or old and broke, so he's used the money he saved for his trip to Ireland to buy a farm near my father's."

"He quit his job at Little Giant?"

"Not yet. We've got to save up some money first."

Polly dug the toe of her boot into the rich black soil beneath their feet. "This dirt is the real gold in these mountains."

"That's what John says." She hesitated. "Polly, anyone can see you love the soil. Why didn't you start a farm instead of a boarding house?"

"Warrens is snowbound six months a year. The growing season's too short."

"Sell the boarding house," Bertha said impulsively. "And Charlie can sell his saloon. That will give you enough to buy a farm in Grangeville. Near us."

Polly laughed. "Charlie love gambling too much to leave his saloon, and I love Charlie too much to leave him."

Mary Dawson, eyes red and hair uncombed, greeted them at the door. "Oh Polly, Bertha, thank God you've come. I've tried everything I know and she's still burning up. I'm afraid the baby will catch it."

"Don't worry," Polly soothed, setting down the heavy basket on a table piled high with bottles, dishes, pans, and uneaten food. "I use this tea many times and it always bring the fever down."

While Polly unpacked and poured the herb tea into a bowl, Mary rocked the fretting baby and picked ineffectually at the clutter.

TWENTY

Bertha took the baby and led Mary out of the room. "You rest now. Polly and I will take care of everything."

Polly slipped the candied coconut into her apron pocket and carried the bowl of tea into the curtained alcove behind the stove. How small the child looked under the pile of heavy quilts. And how flushed. She laid a hand on Katy's forehead. Hot as a cookstove after a day of baking.

The child's eyes fluttered open, green and fever bright. "Polly? I want Polly."

"Polly is here," she said, brushing the tendrils of damp hair from Katy's face. "And Polly bring medicine to make you feel better."

Katy pushed her face into the pillow. "No. No more medicine," she whimpered.

Polly sat down beside her. "You get better, I take you to fly kite."

Katy twisted back to face Polly. "A dragon kite?"

Polly, nodding, dipped the porcelain spoon into the tea.

"As big as the one you made for Mike?"

"Bigger," she promised, holding the spoonful of tea in front of Katy's swollen, blistered lips.

Katy swallowed the tea. Her face puckered. "I don't like it."

Polly dipped the spoon into the tea, then turned it so the handle touched Katy's lips. "Watch the muddy brown water go down the sluice box into the gully," she said, tipping it so the liquid poured through the curved handle into Katy's mouth.

Katy giggled. "Again."

Polly obeyed, again and again, until the herb tea was almost gone.

"No more," Katy said, sliding under the quilts.

Polly reached into her pocket and took out a piece of coconut candy. She laid it on her lap where Katy could see it. "For you when you finish."

The child peered into the bowl. "Okay," she agreed grudgingly.

Swiftly, Polly administered the rest of the tea and popped the candy into the child's mouth. While Katy sucked contentedly, Polly brushed out the tangled hair and changed the soiled nightgown.

She pinched the child's cheeks lightly with both hands. "Now you sleep, and when you wake up, I give you surprise," she said, tucking the child back under the quilts.

Watching the tiny, fever-ravaged body relax into sleep, Polly felt a familiar flash of regret that the children she nursed so lovingly were never her own, and she began a lullaby her mother had sung, beating back the shadow on her happiness with song.

Above the melody, she heard the whirring and honking of geese flying overhead. She imagined the birds dipping and soaring with her song, keeping their perfect wedge-shaped formation as they flew south for the winter.

TWENTY

She loved the winter. The pure whiteness of the snow. The trouble-free months of isolation from the outside world. The funny, strange activities. Like the Hocum Felta Association whose members each took turns trying to be as funny as possible while the rest of the club attempted to remain poker faced until, finally, someone's mouth would twitch, issuing short, sharp splutters which eventually exploded into helpless laughter.

Hoofbeats thundered outside, breaking Polly's reverie, drowning the quiet inside sounds of Bertha tidying the kitchen, Katy's uneven breathing, Polly's song.

The pounding hooves stopped. A door burst open. Slammed. And suddenly a white-faced Bertha was standing beside her, saying, "Come quick, Charlie's been shot bad."

TWENTY-ONE

Too stunned to speak, Polly allowed Bertha to lead her outside, Benson to pull her up behind him on his sweat-soaked horse. He kicked the tired beast into a gallop.

Shot bad, Bertha had said. What did that mean, Polly wanted to ask, but she did not dare, for the exhausted horse told her Benson had looked elsewhere before he found her. How long had it been since Charlie was shot? What if she was too late?

She had to talk. Anything rather than think of Charlie lying in a pool of blood. Dying. Possibly dead.

"Where?" she asked.

"In the head."

Polly closed her eyes, shutting off the images and thoughts his words conjured. "No. Where is Charlie?"

"In the saloon."

The drum of hoofbeats, her own loudly beating

heart, and screaming fears made it impossible for Polly to hear properly. "Where?" she repeated.

"Saloon. The room in the back."

He had said saloon. The room in the back. But who would shoot Charlie there? And why?

As though she had spoken the questions out loud, she heard Benson shout, "Johnny Cox did it."

Johnny Cox? That didn't make sense. Or did it? She remembered how Cox had swaggered into camp the night before with his poke full of dust from a cleanup on Crooked Creek. Intent on a bust, he had gone straight to Charlie's saloon to drink and play poker. But after he had lost two hundred and fifty dollars, Charlie had refused to play another hand until Cox sobered up. Had Cox thought Charlie was trying to cheat him? Denying him a chance to win his money back? She had seen men get shot for less. And she knew Cox was a bad man to fool with. Yet she could not believe he had shot Charlie. Not when he had asked Charlie to watch out for him. To make sure he didn't lose his whole poke.

"Charlie is too good a shot. You sure he's hurt?"

She felt Benson's body twist around, his spurs dig into the horse. "Charlie was taking a nap so Cox had the drop on him," he shouted. "Told Charlie he'd give him the time it took to roll a cigarette to get the money out of the safe or he'd shoot Charlie's eye out. There was no way for Charlie to get his irons from the end of the couch so he called Cox's bluff. Shut his eyes and rolled over. That's when Cox shot him."

Polly listened disbelievingly. Only the mob of angry miners outside the saloon convinced her of the truth.

"Don't worry Polly," the sheriff said, helping her dismount. "Cone's gone after Cox like a coyote after a jackrabbit."

He pushed wide the swinging doors and followed Polly into the saloon, his footsteps reverberating in the unnatural quiet. "He'll get that killer, make no mistake."

Killer? Then she was too late. Her knees wobbled like those of a newborn calf, and she was glad of the knob to lean on when she opened the door to the back room.

There was blood everywhere. On the couch. The floor. Its pungent, metallic odor overcoming the familiar smells of tobacco and liquor. How could there be so much blood and Charlie still live?

He was lying on the couch. Covered. Except for his face, yellow gray and waxy. A death mask. Polly signaled the sheriff she wanted to go in alone.

She leaned over Charlie. A black hole gaped beneath his right eye and beads of sweat trickled between ridges of clotted blood. There was a dry rattling. The quilt rose imperceptibly, then fell. He was alive!

"Charlie!"

Beneath the quilt she saw movement, a feeble

groping. She lowered the quilt and took his hand. "First thing we take you home and clean you up," she said.

"No. Stay here." Blood seeped out of his mouth into his beard.

"Shhh. Don't talk now."

"Must. Running out of time." His eyes, dark caverns of pain, opened. "I love you Polly. Marry me."

The constriction in her chest was unbearable. She lifted a corner of the quilt and wiped the blood from his lips, his beard. "Shhh. Later. We talk later."

"The saloon, the gold in the safe, everything I have is yours."

Struggling, he lifted his hand a few inches before it dropped back onto the couch. His eyes rolled and Polly, following his gaze, saw they were not alone. From out of the shadows, Pony Smead, the justice of the peace, stepped forward.

"Doctor. Charlie need a doctor."

"Troll's already sent to Grangeville for one, but even riding hard it will be night again before he gets here. By then it might be too late."

She bit her lips to keep back the sob that choked in her throat.

"No one I know in Warrens would want to cheat you," Smead continued. "But you know what the law is. It'll be safer if you marry."

Polly sank to her knees beside Charlie. "You

listen to me, Charlie. You get better. I promise you."

His eyes, black with defeat, closed. "No."

She laid her head against his chest. "You got to let me try."

He did not answer.

She turned to Smead. "You find Troll. Then take the door down and use it for a stretcher to carry Charlie home. I will go ahead and get ready."

Stumbling back through the crowd to her boarding house, Polly closed her ears to the remarks, angry and sympathetic, forcing herself to think only of what she would need. Something to clean the wound. Cloths. Plenty of clean cloths. And herbs. To stop the bleeding. To replenish the blood he'd already lost. To give him strength. Quickly, she gathered all she had.

She ran over to Charlie's and put a kettle of water on to boil. Smead and Troll eased Charlie onto the bed. Polly poured some whiskey into a glass and gently lifted Charlie's head.

"Drink this," she said, holding the glass to his lips.

She tipped the glass. The liquor spilled into his mouth and over his beard. He did not swallow.

"He's unconscious," Troll said.

"I help Smead hold Charlie while you get the bullet out," she told him.

"Don't you think we should wait for the doctor?" Troll asked.

Polly, taking a reading of Charlie's feeble pulse, shook her head. "We lose too much time already."

Still Troll hesitated. "We have no instruments."

Polly glanced around the cabin. She picked up her crochet hook. "Use this."

Troll paled. "A crochet hook?"

"You and Smead hold Charlie. I will clean," she said.

She worked silently. Digging. Daubing. Staunching. Desperately pretending the tortured moans did not come from Charlie. The hole was closer to the eye and larger than she had thought, and the crochet hook sank deeper and deeper, but she could not find the bullet. Bits of flesh and splintered bone gleamed whitely on cotton swabs blackened with powder and blood. The pile grew. Blood spurted freshly from the wound. She packed it with a poultice of herbs and fresh cloths. The wound was clean, but the doctor would have to get the bullet.

"Thank you. I will wait with Charlie for the doctor," she told Smead and Troll.

Wearily Polly closed the door behind the men and sank into the chair beside the bed. Charlie groaned.

"Polly's here," she soothed. "You okay."

He tossed restlessly. She cradled him in her arms. He quieted. Dusk deepened into night. The saloons closed. There was a burst of footsteps and noisy talk, the soft whinnying of horses. Hoofbeats. A door slammed. Crickets chirped. A coyote howled. The lamp spluttered, went out. Intending to relight it, Polly half rose.

"No," Charlie moaned. "No."

She stayed, not moving, willing her breath, her strength, to flow into Charlie. Light, dusky gray, filtered through the windows. She heard the town come to life. Still she did not move. Sunshine, honey golden, flooded the room, warming her, and through her, Charlie. Friends came and went. But concentrating on pouring all her strength, her life into Charlie, Polly did not speak, did not move. Then, as dusk came again, she heard horses pounding to a halt. Footsteps. The doctor.

Troll held the lamp above Dr. Bibby as he worked on Charlie. The doctor's three-hundred-pound bulk cast deep shadows, and Polly lit a second lamp and brought it close. On the packing crate beside the bed, metal and bits of bone glowed like red hot coals.

The doctor, his giant body sagging from exhaustion, dropped his instruments into the basin of hot water. "The ball must have hit the cheekbone and split. I can only find half of it."

"What does that mean?" Troll asked.

"Unless Bemis' system is strong enough to expel

the other part of the bullet, the fragment will induce blood poisoning."

He washed his hands and dried his instruments. Polly set the lamp down. "You finish, you will not look for it?" she asked, alarmed.

The doctor shook his head. "I've probed as deep and as long as I dare."

"No," Polly protested. "You can find it. I know. You're tired. You rest. Then you look again."

Dr. Bibby snapped his case shut. "I've done all I can."

"No," Polly denied. "You're the best doctor. I know. I never see you before, but I hear. I know one time you need special instrument for operation at ranch and you make it yourself in the blacksmith shop. You can do anything. I know. I hear."

"And I've heard what an excellent nurse you are. Too good for me to lie to."

He took a bottle of laudanum from the table. "The wound will probably be fatal, but this will ease the pain and make the going easier for the both of you."

She backed away, refusing to take the bottle he offered. "No. He will get well, I tell you. He will."

TWENTY-TWO

Polly had smelled the stink of death before. Only a faint, teasing whiff two days ago, the sickeningly sweet odor of rotting flesh had become distinct. Soon it would begin to cling, becoming as impenetrable and inescapable as a shroud.

She fell to her knees beside Charlie. He was lying as he had since the shooting. Silent and inert. Only now the gaping hole in his cheek oozed yellow green pus. She laid her hand on his.

How often she had felt this hand. This hand which danced in the air when Charlie spoke, split logs for her woodbox, and turned fallen leaves to study the insects below. This hand, familiar and smooth as worn leather, which stroked her body, playing it like he played his violin, making it come alive with joy and longing.

There was a knock at the door. Polly ignored it. She wanted to see no one. Except Charlie. Charlie come alive again, his deep-throated laughter washing over her like clear spring water.

TWENTY-TWO

Behind Polly, the door opened. She recognized Bertha's light tread, but she did not turn.

"Have you heard? Mr. Cone's arrested Cox! He tracked Cox to Salmon Meadows, found he'd sold his horse and gone by stage to Weiser, so followed him there. Someone in Weiser had seen Cox catch a train, but no one knew where the train was headed. Luckily, Mr. Cone heard it was paytime in Pocatello. He guessed Cox would go there to try and pick up some cash gambling, and that's where he was! Going by the name of Eaton, but Mr. Cone got him."

Reaching Polly, Bertha's excited chatter trailed off into silence. She knelt beside her friend. "What is it?"

Polly laid Charlie's hand back beneath the quilt. "It's three weeks, more, since the shooting. The hole should begin to heal, not have pus and smell."

"What does Mr. Troll say?"

"He think Charlie will die."

Bertha winced. "What about Li Dick?"

"He give me special white powder, mold, to kill infection. Always before on other people it work. But not on Charlie."

"Does Li Dick know why?"

"He say the same as Dr. Bibby. The bullet inside Charlie make his blood poison."

"Then we have to find the rest of the bullet," Bertha said simply.

Polly fell back on her heels. "How? I look, Dr. Bibby look. We cannot find it."

Bertha gazed thoughtfully at Charlie. After a few minutes, she turned back to Polly and said, "It was right after the shooting when you and Dr. Bibby tried to find the bullet, and you both looked in Charlie's cheek. Didn't Dr. Bibby say the bullet could work its way to another part of Charlie's body?"

"But where?" Polly, exasperated by Bertha's naive, well-meaning questions, snapped. "I cannot cut Charlie open to see."

"No, but you can feel."

Polly closed her eyes. An overwhelming tiredness pressed her down and she could not move. She felt Bertha's hands on her shoulders.

"Polly, you were only a girl when your father sold you, but you were strong. Strong enough to cross the ocean to a new world. Strong enough to forge a new life for yourself. Aren't you strong enough to keep fighting for the life of the man you love?"

Wearily Polly opened her eyes. "My strength is all used up."

"You've both hung on this long, you can't give up now," Bertha pleaded, her passion as sincere as Polly's had been when she had cried, "He will get well. He will."

She had believed it then. Now she was not

sure. The doctor had been right about the laudanum Charlie would need to escape the pain. Was he also right about the blood poisoning? Certainly Troll and Li Dick agreed.

Bertha walked to the foot of the bed. "Charlie was lying down when Cox shot him," she said slowly. "And Dr. Bibby said the bullet hit the cheekbone. Is it possible the other part went past the bone and down to the back of the head?" She walked back around until she stood opposite Polly. "Let's turn him and see."

Unable to prevent the tiny flicker of hope Bertha's words had ignited, Polly leaned heavily on the bed and pushed herself upright. Together, they turned Charlie. She probed the skull beneath his hair. Nothing. Her fingers worked their way down to his neck. His skin, fiery hot to her touch, was moist. How thin he had become. All bone and flacid muscle. She felt the faint beginnings of a lump. Bone? She brushed aside his hair. Near the center of his neck the skin swelled discolored over the beginnings of a hard, ungiving ridge.

She looked at Bertha. "Is this bone or bullet?"

"It's close to the backbone but off center from it," Bertha said, feeling in the area Polly pointed to. Her eyes brightened. "I think you've found it. Shall I fetch Mr. Troll?"

He had been unwilling to clean the wound without the doctor. How would he feel about digging for a bullet fragment they only believed was there? Would he insist on sending for Dr. Bibby again?

"I do it," Polly said, assembling Charlie's razor, scissors, clean cloths, herbs, and Li Dick's mold on the dry goods box beside Charlie's bed.

Bertha put the kettle on to boil. "What about Li Dick?"

"He does not believe in cutting people," she said tersely, testing the edge of the razor.

She reached for the strop which hung above the washstand and moved the razor across the leather, back and forth, back and forth, the smooth, rhythmic stroking a soothing contrast to the rapid beating of her heart.

"Won't we need help holding Charlie down?"

Polly tested the edge of the razor. It needed no further sharpening. She dropped the strop. "Charlie is full of laudanum. But to be safe, we can tie him down."

They tied him down with sheets twisted into soft ropes. Polly gathered back his hair from around the ridge of skin, cutting and shaving the soft tufts she could not pin. She scrubbed her hands in the basin of scalding hot water, turning them a mottled red.

Bertha stationed herself across from Polly, hot water and cloths on the stool beside her.

A loud croaking broke the hard silence, followed by another and another. Cranes migrating south.

Croaking orders down the line. Cranes. Birds of Death.

"Ready?" Bertha prompted.

Polly, shuddering at the omen, hesitated. Then deliberately she wiped her hands, dipped the razor into the water and wiped it with a cloth soaked in whiskey. "Ready," she breathed.

The razor sank into Charlie's neck, letting loose a gush of red black blood which soaked the pads of white cloth Bertha held ready. Polly dug deeper. The tip touched something hard. Bullet or bone? She withdrew the razor and forced a finger into the hole she had made, trying to ignore the blood spurting over everything. She felt sweat beading her forehead. A wave of faintness washed over her. She forced her finger deeper. It hit something solid. Something small and smooth. Or was it blood that made it slick? She crooked her finger around the object but could not move it. She would have to use the razor to dislodge it.

She withdrew her finger and wiped it clean on the towel Bertha passed her, then picked up the razor. Let it be bullet and not bone, she prayed, easing the razor back into the wound. She felt a slight movement beneath the razor. Her own trembling, Charlie moving, or the bullet loosening? She heard Charlie groan deeply. She would have to hurry.

"Hush," she soothed, as much for herself as Charlie. "I almost done."

She probed deeper, forcing the razor against the bit of hardness, jiggling it slightly. Drops of sweat splashed from her forehead onto her hands. Should she have waited for the bullet to surface on its own? Gritting her teeth, she forced the razor against the hardness and pushed up. Charlie groaned.

"You have it," Bertha said.

Through a haze of moving gray dots, Polly withdrew the razor and bullet fragment. She dropped them into the basin of water. Pink swirls floated from the razor and bullet fragment, turning the colorless water into deepening shades of red, like the sky at dawn.

Again Charlie groaned. Polly quickly rinsed her hands, dried them, and mixed a poultice which she packed into the wound. "You okay now Charlie," she whispered. "You okay."

TWENTY-THREE

Polly looked up from the gold pin Bancroft had asked her to make for his daughter, Caroline. A simple pick and shovel, it did not require enough concentration to distract her from her concern for Charlie.

Still weak, but completely healed, he sat hunched close to the stove, smoking his pipe, his forehead creased with worry   Worry about what? Though he had not been to the saloon since the shooting, business had continued brisk, so he could not be fretting about money. The stream of visitors was constant, so he could not be lonely. And he was not a vain man, so it could not be the horribly disfiguring scar, red and raw beneath his right eye. Then why was he becoming increasingly withdrawn?

The off-key strains of a violin tuning up sounded faintly outside the tightly closed windows of Charlie's cabin. A flute quavered, followed by a series of disjointed spasms from an accordion.

Incoherent caroling mixed with drunken laughter rose above the sounds of the orchestra.

Polly pushed back her stool and walked to the window. Her breath added to the opaque film created by the steamy warmth. She lifted her apron and wiped a pane clear. Ice crystals frosted the outside corners of the glass and a layer of fresh snow covered the town, but the night was clear, and she looked expectantly in the direction of Charlie's saloon.

Since the Christmas Eve dance had broken up two days ago, the Old Crowd Club had been using the saloon to celebrate, and now they were spilling out onto the snow, reeling in a drunken procession. Pony Smead, the torch bearer, keeled over. His torch, fizzling in the snow, was seized by John Divine.

Polly turned from the window. "They will never make it all around the camp," she laughed.

Charlie, tamping his pipe, gave no indication he had heard her. He knocked out the unsmoked tobacco, refilled the bowl, tamped it down, knocked it out again.

Polly stoked up the remains of the pine knots alight in the stove. She rummaged in the wood box Taylor was keeping filled and added more kindling, a small log. The fire crackled to life, and she inhaled deeply, relishing the fragrant wood smoke.

"Remember the winter of '88 when it was so cold the horses freeze standing up and you let the fire die? By morning your breath make icicles on your beard, all across the blanket and under your nose," she chuckled.

The words fell like pebbles into the tense silence. She wiped her hands on her apron, leaving sooty streaks. "I know something is bothering you, Charlie. Why don't you tell me?"

"It's nothing," he said, playing with his beard, the tender flesh around his scar. "I just want to say something and I don't know how to begin."

Polly massaged his back. Beneath her fingers she felt him seething, like a pot of boiling water. "You know you can say anything, I will not mind."

He refilled his pipe, stopped, let the tobacco spill unheeded, took a deep breath, and blurted. "I haven't forgotten I asked you to marry me the day I was shot."

"I know you say that to protect me," Polly said, carefully keeping her fingers kneading in an even rhythm. "But you are well now, so there's no need."

"You don't understand," Charlie countered, face flushed, hands fidgeting with bits of spilled tobacco. "I love you, Polly. I want to marry you."

He was serious. But why? After all these years. She put her hands over his, stilling his twitching fingers. "We fine like we are."

"What about children? If we don't marry, we can't have children."

She laughed. "I'm thirty-eight. In China, I be a grandmother."

Charlie laughed with her. "So here you'll be a mother!"

Polly walked over to the washstand and straightened the towels. "No."

"Why not? Plenty of women have children in their thirties, forties even. Look at old Mrs. B. Her last child, what's his name, the fourteenth one, you know the one I mean, you helped birth him. Why, when he was born, she must have been close to fifty!"

So it was children he wanted. Why? Because he had come so close to death? For all their talk, their professed frankness with each other, this was the one subject they had never discussed.

Stalling for time, she emptied the wash basin into the slop bucket. As she poured in fresh water from the pitcher for rinsing, images crowded in on Polly. The special smell of a baby. The warmth of a child's arms wrapped around her legs, her neck. The trust in their eyes. The emptiness in her arms when she returned a child to its mother.

She swilled, emptied, and polished the basin dry. "No, Charlie. Not me."

"You mean you can't?"

For a moment Polly was tempted to let him believe that. But she had not lied to him before. Not even when she was Hong King's slave. She would not begin now. "I mean I will not have children because I do not want children."

"I can't believe that. You love children. You

take care of them when they're sick, play with them when they're well. Every time I turn around you seem to have a baby in your arms or pulling at your skirts."

"Other people's children. Not mine." She swallowed hard, her throat a raw lump of pain. "I decide long ago."

Charlie's voice softened. "I can understand why you didn't want children when you were Hong King's slave. Or even these last years. But if we marry, it'll be different."

Polly stared unseeing out of the window. "I know what people call men with Indian wives. Squaw men. They do not live in town and not with the Indians. They belong nowhere. Their children too. Strangers to their father's people and their mother's."

"You're not Indian, Pol."

"It's the same."

"No, not at all. The white people in Warrens have never treated Chinamen badly. Doesn't everyone call A Sam Mayor of Warrens? And in the eighties, during the height of the troubles, when the League was trying to run Chinamen out of Idaho, Warrens stayed peaceful."

They were the same arguments, almost the same words A Sam had used when Li Dick had warned of trouble. But even as Charlie spoke, she felt the same unease, the same pull of the tightrope and wash of loneliness that had come over her during the Fourth of July dance.

She felt his hands on her shoulders, turning her around. "And if there were trouble, don't you know I'd protect you and the children?"

Her fingers reached up to smooth out the deep furrow between his eyes. "I know you try. Just like my father try. But he not save me from the bandits."

TWENTY-FOUR

The stiff pose captured on the pasteboard by the studio photographer could not hide the obvious pride and joy radiating from the happy parents: John Long holding Edward, the first born, already a year old, and Bertha holding Mary, the new baby.

Polly pointed to Mary's lacy dress and bonnet peeping from beneath layers of finely crocheted shawls. "That's the same dress I made for Edward," she told Li Dick proudly.

His cabin was so small that, seated across from each other, their knees almost touched. Nevertheless, he set down his long-stemmed Chinese pipe and leaned closer, his tongue clicking the appropriate noises of admiration Polly demanded.

She rewrapped the photograph carefully in paper and slipped it back into her pocket. "It's been two years since Bertha and John moved to their farm in Grangeville, but I still find myself walking halfway across Warrens Meadow to the Little Giant Mine for a visit before I remember."

"Seems to me there are other things you've forgotten too."

"Don't start that again."

Li Dick relit his pipe. The smell of tobacco mingled with the fragrance of the herbs and roots hanging from the ceiling. "I can't seem to get through to you. The new law from Washington requires all Chinese laborers to register or face deportation." His right hand sliced the air between them. "There are no exceptions."

"If I register and admit I was smuggled in, I'll be deported. If I don't register and I'm found out, I'll be deported. But if I don't register and I'm not found out, I'll live like I've lived for the last twenty-one years."

"You think because we're high up in the mountains the government won't come after you? When they wanted the Sheepeater Indians they sent troops up here to chase them down. They can do the same to us."

She thought of the naked, unreasoned anger of the government troops unleashed against the Sheepeaters who had sought refuge in the high-timbered mountains near Warrens, the willingness of the townspeople to join the battle. "That was different. The Sheepeaters had murdered two white men."

"Only a few committed the murders. The troops went after them all. The whole tribe. And got them. Just like they can get you."

Polly forced a little laugh. "You're as vinegar-faced as a hired mourner."

"And you're behaving like a fool hen." He shook his pipe at her. "If you're so safe in Warrens, why did Bemis have to build your boarding house for you? Why do you have to keep it in his name?" He set his pipe down.

"Look, you and Bemis have lived together almost eighteen years. You're husband and wife by common law. A five-minute ceremony, a piece of paper, and you're safe from deportation forever."

"Leave Charlie out of it," Polly said, twisting the heavy gold buttons Charlie had made her.

Fists pounded against the door, shaking the bundles of herbs, showering Polly and Li Dick with bits of dried leaves and dust.

"Li Dick, open up! It's me, Bemis!"

Li Dick unbolted the door. Charlie and Talkington, crouching low to avoid damaging the herbs, squeezed through the narrow opening. Snow blew in from small drifts piled up against the cabin, and Li Dick quickly slammed the door behind them. The bottles, jars, and tins crowding the shelves that lined his cabin shook and rattled.

"There's a Chinaman, a stranger come in to winter, who's in a jackpot. He's been accused of stealing a pair of boots from a white man," Charlie said.

Li Dick nodded. "I already went up to jail to see him. Mr. Skinner said the men who brought A Foo in threatened to hang him if he did not return the boots, but A Foo insists he did not take them."

Polly slid off the packing crate. "I take him some supper."

"He's not in the jail. I just checked," Talkington said. "Some men Skinner had never seen before came and took him away. They told Skinner they just wanted to scare the truth out of the Chinaman, but they haven't come back. I'm afraid they've gone and done something stupid."

Polly pulled on coat and gloves. "We go look for them."

"No, you go back to your place or mine," Charlie said. "Li Dick, Talkington, and I will take care of this."

"Sometimes men will listen to a woman, not other men." She traced the scar on Charlie's cheek. "I don't want you to risk another shooting," she added softly.

Li Dick gathered lanterns, a knife. "They'll be gone by now."

"The men weren't on horseback. I figure they didn't intend to take the Chinaman far," Talkington said.

He opened the door. "Skinner says he saw them headed for the river."

Their lanterns held high, they walked in the direction Talkington suggested. Snow, like a fresh lime coating, covered the garbage strewn mud paths that twisted through the huddle of window-less shacks, purging the air of familiar odors, smothering the usual cacophony of night sounds.

It was like a ghost village, Polly thought, goosebumps rising beneath her warm flannel dress and wool coat. A ghost village hoping to escape notice, hence wrath.

Their boots crunched through the thin crust of ice above the first snow of the season. Loose snow rippled like sea sand.

"We can cover more ground if we fan out," Li Dick suggested.

"It's safer if we stick together," Charlie said.

Polly plucked Charlie's sleeve. "Li Dick is right."

Reluctantly, Charlie agreed and they spread out, leaving the town behind them.

Closer to the river, the snow was slick with treacherous ice patches. Wind whipped Polly's skirts, twisting them around her legs, and each step became a battle for balance. The sky, pitch black, threatened a second storm, but she needed support more than she needed light. She set down her lantern.

With one arm, she gripped the ice-sheathed trunk ahead and stepped carefully toward it. The next tree was too far to reach with her hands, but she could grab a branch. Her gloved hands crushed the tiny, glittering icicles shrouding the branch, and she edged forward without falling. Slowly, laboriously, with wind-carried spray stinging her face with fine hard crystals of ice, she worked her way from one tree to the next, leaving the pale glow of her lantern farther and farther behind.

A quarter moon, struggling from behind black clouds, cast gloomy shadows through thickly intertwined branches. From below came the sounds of water smashing against rocks, pulling fallen branches, debris. Closer, she heard a faint rustling. Almost a sigh, it might be the wind or a small wood animal. But the moaning. Was that the wind? Or a human, a man in pain?

She stopped. Not far from her, Charlie's, Li Dick's, and Talkington's lanterns bobbed, their twinkling lights reassuring her of help nearby. But in her own immediate area, there were only shadows.

A snowshoe hare skimmed across the snow, its white winter coat startling in the darkness. A wolf howled, the sound wild and drawn out. Owls hooted. The moon disappeared and the black sky released its snow, dusting the pine branches. She would have to start back before the light powdering became a blinding whirl.

Head bent against the wind, she turned and worked her way cautiously up the ice slick slope toward the barely visible glow of her lantern. A broken branch dangled dangerously. She pushed it aside.

TWENTY-FOUR

It swayed stiffly. Not a broken branch, but a
broken man wrapped in a new shroud of feathery
white flakes.

TWENTY-FIVE

The dream, when it came, was always the same. The tightrope stretched taut. Herself edging forward. Tired. Anxious to reach the end.

She could not see the place she was struggling to reach. But she could feel its contentment, a sense of repletion. And then, without warning, a branch snapped, knocking her off balance. She fell. The bark peeled off the branch, and she found herself staring into eyes, red and bulging, in a face swollen black, the tongue, distended, choking off a silent scream.

"No," Polly shouted. "No."

Charlie shook her. "Wake up, Pol."

A match scratched against flint and Polly became aware of a sudden glare beyond the darkness of eyelids squeezed shut. Hands straightened her twisted nightgown, stroking, soothing, forcing the dream to recede until she finally dared open her eyes.

There were their two chairs pulled up to the

stove. Charlie's fiddle. The tablecloth she had embroidered. Her plaid dress, gold buttons gleaming, hanging on a nail. Charlie's corduroy pants and flannel shirt tossed on a chair. His boots. Pipe.

Charlie picked up the quilt from the floor where Polly had kicked it, tucking it around her. "Pol, the hanging was terrible, but it's been eight months."

"The men who hang A Foo are still out there."

"They were outsiders Skinner had never seen before."

"Now snow is gone, they can come back. Why you think Chinatown is almost empty?"

"For the same reason white men are leaving Warrens. There's no gold and times are bad."

"Maybe. But Li Dick say, and you know it's true, bad times are when trouble always begin."

Charlie smoothed the hair from Polly's forehead. "Let's close down the saloon and boarding house and take a trip."

"What?"

"There's a place I want to show you."

"Where?"

He smiled. "Not far, just a day's ride. But I can't tell you about it, you have to see it for yourself."

His eyes shone with excitement, like a young man's. A young man with a secret.

"Okay," she agreed. "We go."

Polly took a last bite of the trout Charlie had caught earlier. She had coated it in yellow corn-meal and fried it crisp, serving it sizzling hot with the dandelion greens she had found while Charlie fished. The fresh, tender meat contrasted perfectly with the crunchy casing, and she glowed with the satisfaction that comes at the end of a meal enjoyed. Careful not to disturb Charlie, napping in the shade of a mahogany bush, she gathered the tin plates, forks, and pans and headed for the river to wash.

How deceptive the river was. At first, near Warrens, it had been only a faint rustle. Then, gradually, as they descended the gorge, the rustling had become a rushing roar. Now, at the water's edge, she could see arcs of broken rainbows curving across falls, foam beads glittering like fiery opals, awesome in their colorful beauty. But it was the sound the water made as it crashed against the huge rocks rising dark and treacherous from the Salmon's depths that amazed Polly the most.

A few yards away, a creek, a mere silver streak winding through stands of firs and pines, broadened into shallows, then suddenly narrowed, gushing into the deep, boiling eddies of the Salmon. Across the river, a second, larger creek did the same. And the sound of all the tumbling, boiling water was mesmerizing, washing away any thought of the troubled world beyond the canyon walls.

TWENTY-FIVE

Impulsively Polly bent and took off her shoes and stockings. The ice cold water lapped against her toes as she strolled along the sand bar, adding her own footprints to the peppered impressions and trailing quill lines of porcupines and, farther on, the tracks of bobcats, minks, otters, and deer.

At the end of the bar, she turned and went back, scuffing up the hot sand, feeling it slide off her feet. She dipped the dishes and pan into the river. A beaver stuck its sleek, dripping face up from the water and eyed Polly inquisitively. Playfully, she splattered it with water. For a moment, it did not move, staring, defiant. Then it dove out of sight. Chuckling, she finished the washing, laid the dishes, pan and forks beside the dying embers of the cooking fire, and dragged her saddle near Charlie.

It was hard to believe that this canyon, so wild and secluded, was only eighteen miles from Warrens, but she could fully understand why the Mallicks, the Nez Perce family across the river, had chosen it to farm. The land, a wilderness of cheat grass, vicious nettles, sumac, and prickly blackberry thickets, was free for the taking; the soil rich, the growing season ample.

She stretched out, her head pillowed in the satin smoothness of her saddle. Above her, in a pocket of the canyon wall, mountain sheep searched for grass, their slate-colored hides barely discernible against the rock. Closer, on a rocky outcrop streaked with bands of grass and trees, she found the big head and horns of a ram feeding, and near it, two brown spots, one larger than another, a ewe and her lamb. They saw her, but did not run, continuing to eat, confident of their safety. All around them dragonflies flashed. Smaller insects hummed. A squirrel scampered up a nearby trunk rich with yellow and green lichen. The sun felt warm, the peace palpable.

"You see why I couldn't tell you about this canyon, why I had to show you?" Charlie said.

Polly, suffused with a sense of contentment she had never known before, rolled over. "Let's stay a few more days."

Charlie propped himself up on his elbow. "Pol, when I asked you to marry me before, you said there was no reason to. But now, with the new law, there is every reason. Let's get married and come here and start a new life together."

Polly catapulted to her knees, showering Charlie with sand. "You don't mind leaving Warrens?"

"It's only a day's ride. I can rent out the saloon, you can rent out your boarding house, and we can always go into town if life gets too dull."

She laughed. "Dull? Too much work on a farm to be dull!"

"Then you agree?"

She pictured the photograph of Bertha's family, only it was she and Charlie with their own babies, children who would know only the joy and peace the canyon offered. After all, hadn't her father and his fathers before him lived in the same village for generations? But her mother, like the other women, had come from another village and, if she had not been sold, there would have come a day when she would have had to leave her family to go to a husband's home and village. And Jim, Li Dick, A Sam, the hundreds of Chinese men in the hold of the ship, in Warrens, and all the other towns and camps, hadn't they left their fathers' villages like Charlie had left his?

The Gold Mountains teemed with men and women on the move, chasing dreams from coast to coast, city to city, mining camp to mining camp. Her dream, the end of the tightrope, was here. But she could not answer for the dreams of the children she and Charlie might have.

She scooped up a handful of sand. It glittered like the copper coins in her father's hands when he had gambled and lost, the gold Charlie had gambled with Hong King and won. And now she too must gamble.

The sand filtered through the cracks of her fingers, sending sand crabs scurrying out of reach. She tightened her hands into fists. How could she bear to lose this canyon, Charlie.

He tipped her chin. "What is it?"

She looked at her twin reflections in his eyes, the one that yearned to say yes, the one that could not. "Children." She shook her head. "No children."

Charlie took her fists, loosening the fingers until her hands lay open in his. "It's you I want, Pol, nothing more."

Her eyes misted, blurring her twin reflections, making them one. "Then yes, Charlie. Oh yes, I marry and come live with you here."

PART FIVE

第五部份

1898-1922

TWENTY-SIX

The ground cherries rustled in their paper shells as Polly tossed them into the five-pound lard bucket beside her. Their first fall in the Salmon Canyon, she had only had the cherries and wild thimbleberries, huckleberries, and blackberries to can. But each year, as her garden expanded and the trees she had planted in her orchard matured, her harvest had increased, and by the time the first snow fell on this, their fourth winter, the shelves that lined her root cellar would be crammed with bottled bear cracklings, plum butter, canned peaches, apricots, garden truck, venison, and grouse.

In addition to fruits and vegetables, she grew her own wheat and ground her own flour to make bread. The single cow and the hens provided all their dairy needs, and she rendered her own grease and made soap from the occasional bear Charlie shot.

On his trips to check on his saloon in Warrens, Charlie traded Polly's produce for the few necessities they could not grow or make, like coal oil, fabric, thread, and shoes. Polly did not accompany Charlie on these trips, for she had sold her boarding house. Everything and everyone she wanted was either already in the canyon or would come to her here.

During the spring, summer, and fall, there were only the occasional prospectors and adventurers Charlie ferried across the river. But in the winter, when the river froze over with huge chunks of ice, ranchers and old friends from Warrens would come. They would stay up all night, getting caught up on news, retelling old stories, playing poker, eating, and drinking whiskey made from her own rye and hops. Then Charlie would bring out his fiddle, and there would be singing and sometimes dancing, and for days, their snug, two-storied log cabin would fairly shake from all the laughter and foot stomping.

"Polly, come here," Charlie called.

Polly tossed a last handful of cherries into the bucket, rose, and stretched, proudly surveying Polly Place. Slender green tips of asparagus peeked above flat gray boulders at the base of the steep canyon slope. Grain hay, sowed to rest the soil, spread a golden aura around long rows of dark green cornstalks, beds of lettuce, cabbage, carrots, turnips, and the special herbs she grew for Li Dick. Roosters strutted among the hens which cackled as they scratched in the straw beside the stable.

Meadowlarks sang above the roar of the river, and from the trees beyond the creek, pheasants drummed on a log.

Across the river, the Mallicks' farm stood empty, for they had left for a homestead near Grangeville where their children could attend school. Polly would like to have been nearer to Bertha and Bertha's children, and a farm anywhere would probably give her many of the same pleasures. The feel of rich soil crumbling between her fingers, the warmth of the sun on her back, the ache of muscles after a day's weeding, the steamy fragrance of cooking fruit, the pungent odor of pickling spices. But only this canyon could infuse her with such deep contentment, and she would never leave it. Never.

"Over here," Charlie said.

She could not see him, but his voice came from the direction of the chestnut and mulberry trees she had planted that spring. Polly walked toward them. A big, bald squash peered out from a few dry, hairy green vines which had fought their way through the willow fence enclosing her garden. She took out her bowie knife and cut the stray squash from the vine, rescuing it from the chipmunks and porcupines which came in the night.

"Just look at this nest of ants," Charlie said from where he lay, belly down, studying the ants scurrying around a mound of pine needles and fallen leaves.

Polly set the squash down beside him and dropped to her knees. An earthworm, half buried in the rich black soil, caught her eye. She plucked it out, dusted it free of clinging dirt, and deposited it in her apron pocket.

"If you work like these ants, I have time to go fishing later," she said, lightly patting the worm wriggling in her pocket.

His blue eyes danced. "You want me to plow?"

They both laughed, remembering their first spring in the canyon and the steer Charlie had purchased to break for the plow. Expecting resistance, he hitched the animal to the top of a fallen tree so that if it ran, the branches would gouge into the earth and stop it. The beast ran as predicted. But the branches, instead of gouging into the earth, slid like runners of a sled over the hard ground and Charlie, too surprised to jump out of the way, was knocked down and pushed under the limbs. When the steer finally stopped, Charlie had emerged clothed only in scratches and bruises. And one sock.

"It's the wrong time of year for plowing," Polly said when she stopped laughing. "But you can help me bring up my buckets of cherries."

He retrieved his hat from beneath a bush and put it on. Two large cabbage leaves covered the crown of the hat, and fluttering over the back of his head and neck was a large white handkerchief fastened to the hat band. Polly, pointing to Charlie's hat, burst into a fresh fit of laughter.

Charlie drew himself up. "This book I read said it's important to shade the neck from the sun." He took a few steps. "See how the handkerchief moves? That keeps a constant current of air passing through to cool the neck and head."

"Charlie, it's October, almost winter, not August," Polly gasped, using her sleeve to wipe the tears streaming down her cheeks.

"I'm trying it out," he said with mock dignity.

"Even in the summer you don't stay out in the sun long enough to need that."

"I will be."

Trying desperately to keep a straight face, Polly said, "Yes?"

"I'm going to rock for gold."

"You give up mining years ago," Polly reminded. "You say it's too much work."

"Maybe your industry is rubbing off on me."

"Good. Then after you take the cherries up to the house, you can chop wood for my wood box and hull the corn."

"Can't. Got to start staking my claim."

"Right today?"

"You remember the prospectors that came down from Buffalo Hump in August, the ones that were in such a hurry they didn't want to stop to eat or talk?"

She nodded.

"Rumor has it the ore they carried will assay enough gold to start a whole new rush."

A chill ran down Polly's spine, raising the soft, downlike hairs at the back of her neck. A rush would mean men pouring into the canyon on their way to the Hump, destroying the peace, the land. And though she was protected by her marriage certificate and her new certificate of residence which Charlie had sent for from the government office in Montana, there was nothing to protect her home, the farm she had carved out of wilderness no one else had wanted. Until now.

"The ranch?"

Charlie waved his hat at her, laughing. "Don't you see? That's why I'm going back to mining. You can't be a partner in a homestead, and you can't own land, but plenty of Chinamen hold claims. So I'll stake out the ranch as a mining claim and file it the next time I go to Warrens."

TWENTY-SEVEN

They worked well together, Charlie fitting the crude wooden box he had made out of a coal oil crate around the tenderfoot's crushed leg and foot, Polly padding the box with cotton ripped out of old quilts, then binding the leg and box in place with long strips of torn sheets.

As soon as she tied the last knot, the boy swung his good leg off the bed.

"No, no," Polly said. "You must rest five weeks, maybe six, before your leg is strong enough for you to leave."

Holding on to the edge of the mattress with both hands, the boy raised himself off the bed. "Haven't you heard about the strike at Buffalo Hump? If I wait six weeks, there'll be no claims left."

He rested his weight on his good leg, took a step, and winced.

Charlie gripped the boy's shoulders and pushed him back on the bed. "You don't know it, but you've got the Angel of the Salmon River caring for you, and if she says five to six weeks before you're fit to move on, that's how long it will be."

The boy propped himself up on his elbows. "But this is a chance in a lifetime."

"You already used up your chance in this lifetime when you tumbled down the mountain and lost your outfit and your horse. If I hadn't happened on you by accident, you would have lost your life too. Don't tempt fate twice," Charlie said, swinging the boy's legs back onto the bed. "Besides, you can't cross the river if I don't row you."

"They say the strike at the Hump is so rich you only need a few days with a shovel and gold pan to get enough dust to be a millionaire!" the boy pleaded.

His eyes, his face, his whole person shone with the same naive hope that had buoyed Polly and all the other men and women crowded into the hold of the ship which had brought her to America, and she knew there was nothing either she or Charlie could say that would deter the boy.

Smiling, she pulled a quilt over him. "With this bad leg, it will take you one week, maybe two to reach the Hump. If you do not die first. On a horse, with Charlie to show you the way, you can get there in two days. So you stay here two weeks, then Charlie will take you."

From the moment Charlie had come home with the tenderfoot across his packhorse instead of a deer, Polly had realized that the winter snows would not protect them from the rush for Buffalo Hump, and Charlie's trip to the Hump with the boy had confirmed it.

The vein of ore was huge, fully visible for five miles, and its course ran down through the Salmon. Despite several feet of snow, more than one hundred prospectors were already living in tents along the vein, and every day more arrived. They came on horseback, often two men on a horse. Or on foot, with huge packs on their backs. And they all had one thought. To have Charlie ferry them across the river so they could climb up to the Hump and stake a claim before all were gone.

The ranch, the only claim Polly and Charlie cared about, was staked out, the claim form completed. But it was not filed, for the ten-foot deep ditch required by law had not been dug.

They had cleared an area near the creek where their sluice boxes would go, and they had started to dig, swinging their picks into the, by then, frost-hardened, ungiving earth. But as the four-foot-square shaft deepened inch by inch, the weather worsened, and Charlie's cough grew more worrisome until Polly insisted he stop.

Coughing and panting, his wet clothes frozen stiff, he refused. "You've heard the men coming through. Grangeville's a madhouse, and Florence and Elk City and a lot of other camps are empty because people are rushing to the Hump. They're staking claims in ten, fifteen feet of snow."

"Most of those claims won't hold up."

The scar from the shooting stood out harshly red in a face gray with exhaustion. "Exactly. This one will," he coughed.

Polly covered Charlie's mittened hands with hers, preventing him from lifting the pick. "You think I care about the claim if this is your grave we are digging?"

That night she wakened to feel Charlie burning with fever. In a voice hoarse from coughing, he complained of tightness in his chest. For days Polly made hot mustard and linseed poultices for his chest, simmered herb teas for him to drink, and brought up kettles of steaming hot water for him to inhale. His cough worsened, his nose bled, and she ran up and down the stairs cleaning the slop bucket, changing the sweat-soaked sheets. Finally, in the second week of illness, his fever broke. But it was almost a month before he was well enough to go downstairs again.

He sat hunched over the stove, puffing on his pipe, staring through frost-crusted windows at a world turned white as mourning. Across the river which crashed and roared beneath slabs of congealed ice, the fires of prospectors camped along Crooked Creek winked, mocking.

Polly rammed her fist into the dough she had

left to rise. While Charlie had demanded her constant attention, she had not had time to think of the ditch left unfinished, the claim not filed. But now, with his recovery assured, fears she had refused to acknowledge surfaced.

She pounded the dough with calloused brown fingers balled into fists, kneading, pressing down unwanted thoughts as well as dough. Then she shaped the formless mass into loaves which would rise and fall and rise again. Like lives.

Was that the reason for the New Year cake families in her village made each year? It was the one time her father supervised the cooking, shutting all the doors just before her mother eased the dough into the huge boiler to steam. Then he would light the incense to time the cooking, hovering as it smoldered into ash. Finally, as he lifted the lid, waving away the cloud of steam which burst out like a winter mist, they would all crowd around, anxious to see if the cake was a fluffy, delicious omen of good luck or a flat portent of disaster.

Polly set the pans of light bread on the stove to rise. Her mother's cake had always risen. Even the New Year before the winter wheat. The New Year before she was sold. It was not luck that determined the rise and fall of cakes or bread or lives, but skill, strength, the right ingredients.

She wiped her floury hands on her apron and wrapped herself up in coat, scarves, boots. She had skill and strength. And she would create the right ingredients.

Alternately urging him to hurry and to walk slowly, Polly led a well-bundled Charlie toward the frozen creek. The wind-whipped mountain slopes glared a painful white against the sunny blue sky, but dark shadows slashed the snow-covered floor of the canyon, and the sharp frosty air, fragrant with wood smoke, stung Charlie's sallow cheeks into a chapped red. From the hen house came the sleepy clucking of chickens jostling in their roosts, and from the stable the tinkle of the cow bell, the restless nickering and pawing of horses.

Their boots crunched in the ice-crusted snow.

"The canyon is not the same when the river is frozen silent," Polly said.

"Makes travel to the Hump easier," Charlie said gloomily, his breath puffing out like smoke.

Polly playfully caught at the wispy streamers of white breath. "The Hump is not the only place people go."

"This winter it is."

"Not you," she said, bringing them to a sudden stop. "You will go to Warrens."

"What for?"

"To file the claim."

TWENTY-SEVEN

Stooping, she dragged away broken pine branches laden with clumps of new snow, revealing a ditch exactly four feet square and ten feet deep.

Charlie gaped. "That's impossible! The ground is frozen solid."

"Not when I dig," Polly chuckled, enjoying Charlie's astonishment. "Each day I build a fire in the hole and warm the top of the ground. Then I dig. When I reach frozen earth again, I stop and build a new fire."

"This calls for a celebration!" Charlie said.

"Not yet. When you come back from Warrens."

TWENTY-EIGHT

During her twenty-two years in Warrens, Polly
had observed that there were five types of miners.
The happy-go-lucky prospectors, men of few words
who roamed the forests and mountains with
boundless patience and optimism. Placer miners
who drifted from stream to stream, seesawing
between poverty and riches, hardship and hard
living. Promoters, flabby and soft, who were not
above salting samples before assaying in order to
attract investors. Financiers, capitalists who knew
little and cared less about mining and miners, but
whose money bought the machinery, organization,
and engineering necessary for proper development. And hard rock miners, men like John Long,
courageous and reliable, who brought the leavening
influence of wives and children into the camp.

The strike at Buffalo Hump, advertised as "the
greatest gold camp on earth," brought men from all
around the world. Men with the same hopes and
fears, greed and generous good natures, rugged

individuality and prejudices as the ones Polly had observed in Warrens. And at first, during the tense months before Charlie successfully filed the claim for Polly Place, she had felt the tightrope returning. But with the ranch secure, the fears and bad dreams which had returned vanished.

By July of the following year, the only claims left were those invented for sale to suckers, and the steady stream of hopeful men trudging through the canyon on their way to the Hump dwindled to a trickle. But promoters enticed capitalists from the East, and a year later, mill operations were started at the Big Buffalo, Crackerjack, Badger, and Jumbo Mines, and development began in earnest.

Then in July of 1901, there was a new rush, this time for Thunder Mountain. "The gold on that mountain is skin deep," Charlie said scornfully. Nevertheless, optimistic prospectors, miners, and smooth-talking promoters were able to keep rumors and mines alive for almost a decade until a slide in 1909 created a lake, putting Roosevelt, the supply camp, underwater.

Traffic through the canyon shrank back to the occasional prospector and adventurer, and the peace Polly loved so well returned, more satisfying and deeply valued than before.

There were a few permanent changes. In order to keep the claim on the ranch valid, she and Charlie now placered each spring when the creek was at high water. And they had new neighbors, Charles

Shepp and Pete Klinkhammer, who had bought the Mallick's old farm across the river.

They had met Shepp, an old Klondike argonaut, near the start of the Buffalo Hump rush when he filed a claim on the west fork of Crooked Creek and rode down to buy produce from Polly. Two years later, Pete, a young man who had left his parents' Minnesota farm to seek adventure in the West, joined Shepp. Unlike Polly, Pete had wanted to leave farming behind him, but neither the mine nor the brewery company he and Shepp started was successful, and when the Northern Pacific made a survey for running a line through the canyon, they bought Tom Copenhaver's claim on the Mallick farm.

"You think the railroad will come to the canyon?" Polly asked.

Charlie pushed Teddy, their black and white terrier, off his chest and rolled over in the grass. "We'll never see the railroad here."

Teddy scooted over to Polly. She scratched his ears with her left hand, continuing to paint the hen house with her right. "Pete say he and Shepp homestead one hundred thirty-seven acres."

"One hundred thirty-seven," she repeated, shaking her brush for emphasis. "I busy all day with twenty."

Charlie snatched his fiddle out of reach of the drops of carbolic acid and coal oil sprinkling from Polly's brush. He tucked it under his chin. "Don't forget they have two men working the place. You only have yourself. Besides, Pete is less than half your age, and both Shepp and Pete are twice your size," he said, drawing the bow across the strings.

"Pete handle the stock and the team for plowing and haying, but he still do assessment work to bring in cash. Shepp take care of all the garden work by himself and he is also carpenter and cook," she said, squirreling inside the hen house to paint the mite-infested roosts.

"Makes a fellow tired just thinking about it."

Polly stuck her head out. "Not too tired to hunt, I hope. I tell Shepp and Pete since they have so much work, you will hunt fresh meat for us all."

Lifting her hems, damp from the last traces of morning dew, Polly skirted a thorn bush and took Charlie's hand. Clammy. She reached up and felt his forehead. Beneath a fine film of perspiration, it was cold to her touch. He had told her his eyes were weakening and he needed her to sight the game for him to shoot, but he had not said how difficult the climb uphill had become for him.

He coughed. In the aftermath, Polly detected the same rattle that had worried her during his attack of pneumonia the winter of the Buffalo Hump rush.

"You okay?" she asked.

"Fine," he panted, propping his Winchester

against a pine and collapsing onto a soft bed of ferns. "Just need a few minutes to catch my breath."

Polly knelt beside him. "You sure?"

"Polly, I'm sixty-three years old and winded. That's all."

Teddy hurtled back down the steep wall of the canyon. Panting, he threw himself down at Polly's feet.

"See, even Teddy needs a break," he said, stretching out.

Polly leaned back against a fallen log, thoughtfully chewing a blade of sour grass. Beneath them thundered the Salmon. Swollen ten, twenty feet above its summer level, it swept along fallen trees, rolling rocks, the last few blocks of unmelted ice. In the distance, a lone buck rubbed its new antlers against a pine tree, scraping off the velvet, polishing. Closer, on the creek bank, a beaver sat, combing its fur with its toe nails. Everything smelled alive, fresh, newly green.

Teddy, eager to be off again, nuzzled inquiringly, his nose wet and cold against Polly's cheek. She scratched behind his ears, burying her face in his fur. Perhaps Charlie was right and she was just over anxious. Wasn't she almost sixty herself, her hair white, her brown face wrinkled as a walnut, her fingers beginning to gnarl?

"Look," Charlie said, pointing to a golden eagle circling the sky above a rocky ledge.

TWENTY-EIGHT

As Polly's eyes followed Charlie's finger, the huge bird tucked in its wings and dove. When the distance between ledge and bird narrowed, it spread out its wings. Then, barely touching the ledge, it soared back up, its claws weighted down with a yellow bundle.

Charlie stood. He dusted off dirt, bits of twigs and dead leaves. "What is it?" he asked, squinting.

"Some kind of cub I think."

"Any sign of a mother?"

She caught a quick movement on the ledge, but it was far too small to be a grown cat. "No. Maybe another cub."

"Not like a nursing mother to leave her babies, let's go check it out."

TWENTY-NINE

Charlie picked up the cub. "A cougar. She can't be more than six weeks old."

"I make a bottle for her."

"She might refuse cow's milk. Like those motherless lambs you tried to raise," Charlie warned.

But unlike the lambs which had stubbornly locked their jaws against the bottle, letting the milk spill into their tight curls until they reeked of sour milk, weakened, and died, the cougar cub sucked until her stomach bulged, then yawned and stretched. Teddy, his furry brow wrinkled comically, hovered while the cub sniffed at the furniture and the plants outside, turning over pinecones, tossing leaves and feathers, and tumbling over fallen branches. When she strayed, he picked her up by the scruff of her neck and brought her back, dropping her at Polly's feet, and as the cub grew, they romped together, wrestling.

By the time the cottonwoods turned yellow and

gold, the cub was the same size as Teddy. By midwinter, stretched out, she was as big as Polly, and by spring thaw, larger than Charlie. Sitting on the floor, she could reach and eat from the tin plate Polly had nailed onto the table for her, and when she raked her claws along the trunks of trees, the marks ran deep.

"It isn't natural," Shepp said, pointing to the cougar sitting across from him, licking her plate clean.

Polly, coming in from the kitchen, set generous portions of peach cobbler in front of Charlie, Pete, and Shepp. She poured fresh coffee all around. "Amber make you nervous?"

"Any animal that can break a buck deer's neck with a snap of its jaws makes me nervous," Shepp said, digging into the cobbler.

"She won't hurt you."

"Try telling Tom that," Charlie laughed. "He came down from Warrens last week. Got here after dark and before he knew what was happening, Amber had leaped out of a tree, knocked him off his horse, and pinned him to the ground."

"She only want to play."

"Well, get her to play outside," Pete said.

He shoved back his chair and opened the door. Charlie grabbed Amber by the scruff of the neck. She arched her back and hissed. Teddy rose to his haunches and growled protectively.

Charlie dropped back onto his chair. "You get her," he told Polly.

Polly stroked Amber's arched back, smoothing the fur which had bristled. The cat licked Polly's face wetly.

"Outside," she ordered.

Amber padded obediently toward the open door, her claws clicking on the plank floor. Teddy followed. Polly shut the door behind them.

"There, now you feel safe?" she asked the three men.

Grinning sheepishly, they concentrated on their cobblers and coffee. Pete held his mug out for a refill.

"If prohibition goes through, you could take that cat up to Warrens to guard Charlie's saloon from federal officers," he said.

"Only problem is, she'd scare the customers away too," Charlie said. "But no need to worry, winters will be no problem. The officers, no matter how zealous, will never brave twenty-foot drifts, and in the summer, there are telephone lines between most of the ranches, so it'll be easy to give warning of anyone coming in who looks suspicious."

"A telephone's not too different from the crystal set I made," Shepp said. "I could put a line between our two ranches."

"What for?" Polly asked.

"Maybe they're thinking of going back into the brewery business," Charlie said.

Pete shook his head vigorously. "Never!"

"But a telephone could come in handy," Shepp persisted. "Just think, if we have a line, we can call ahead and have Polly get Amber out of the way before we cross the river."

Teddy, his muzzle spiked cruelly with porcupine quills, squirmed under Charlie's firm grip while Polly tugged at the quills with a pair of pliers.

"Poor Teddy," she sympathized. "You think just because Amber can jump a porcupine and eat the quills, you can."

"Maybe Shepp's right," Charlie said.

The quill Polly was pulling snapped off close to the flesh and Teddy whimpered. "You want to get rid of Amber?"

Perspiration from the strain of holding Teddy mottled Charlie's forehead. "No, of course not. I mean about the telephone. Some day, if we really need help, that signal we use, the white towel on the bush, might not be fast enough."

"They get over here plenty quick enough for fish fries."

Charlie coughed. "Polly, be serious. We're not getting any younger, you know."

She worked the broken quill free. "Years, white hair, and wrinkles mean nothing. They're just a way to mark time. Like the rings in a tree.

Uncle Dave Lewis is more than seventy and he live alone on Big Creek and run a pack string and hunt cougars. And Goon Dick is older than that, but every spring he come back all the way from Seattle to placer in Warrens."

She extracted the last quill, dropped the pliers, and rubbed Teddy's nose tenderly. "Sure I need spectacles for close needlework, but I still farm a big garden. And," she added, laughing, "your fingers are still mighty quick with cards and fiddle."

"Look at me," Charlie said. "I mean really look at me and tell me what you see."

The intensity in his voice startled Polly. She released Teddy and studied Charlie's face. Each morning, when she woke beside him, she was surprised anew at the dark smudges beneath pale, watery blue eyes, the thin wisps of hair, the shock of white beard, the way bones protruded under finely wrinkled skin. But then, during the course of the day, when they talked and laughed, he became the same Charlie who had saved her that first night in Warrens, camas blue eyes dancing, coppery hair and beard a blaze of flame, and she allowed herself to forget how easily he tired. How he made fewer and fewer trips into Warrens. How his pale cheeks flushed as afternoon wore into evening. How her cough syrups and herb teas were losing the fight against the cough which had become a part of him.

She looked away. Amber, head lowered, crouched in the grass, creeping along noiselessly, her tawny fur a slither of gold in the waves of green. She leaped on top of Teddy and they tumbled down the slope, a blur of black and white and gold.

Polly had seen the same scene reenacted many times, and it always made her laugh because she knew Teddy saw Amber long before she jumped. But she did not laugh now. For like Amber, she had allowed herself to be fooled. Refusing to acknowledge what her eyes, her years of nursing the sick had told her.

Polly turned to face Charlie. "We tell Shepp yes, we want the telephone," she said.

THIRTY

The sun dipped behind the canyon walls, its afterglow casting a silvery sheen on the bleached roof shingles still steaming from an unexpected afternoon shower. Polly, laughing, wiped her hands clean on a tuft of damp sour grass. She leaned on the lard bucket, half full of chestnuts, and pushed herself upright.

Pete eyed her quizzically.

"When a person start picking up horse nuts instead of chestnuts, it's time to quit," she chuckled.

Pete picked up the two lard buckets of chestnuts. "I'll take these up to the house for you."

Teddy, his gait stiff and awkward, hurried after Polly and Pete. She slowed, partly to accommodate him, partly because her own feet pained her now after a full day's labor.

"Your harvest good?" she asked.

"Better than our first one."

Polly laughed. "I remember. You plant too

early and everything come up and just sit. You have enough seed for ten years!"

She opened the door for him. "You say you pack produce up to the Jumbo tomorrow?"

Pete set the buckets down. "Yes."

"You have room to take a few things to friends for me?"

"Sure."

From the shelves beneath the stairs, Polly brought out jars and bottles, a crocheted cap. "This liniment is for Jessie, the preserves are for Nellie Shultz, and the crocheted cap you give Four-Eyed Timothy to take to his mother in Dixie."

She wrapped them up in clean flour sacks, tucked them into a well-lined coal oil tin, and headed for the kitchen.

"Whoa!" Pete said. "I'm only taking one mule, not a whole string."

"You mean you have no room for sauerkraut I make like your sister teach me?"

"Well now, that'll just go across the river and I didn't say there wasn't room in the boat," Pete said quickly.

Chuckling, Polly wrapped two jars of sauerkraut and added them to the tin. She followed Pete back out onto the porch. "Thank you for bringing the mail. Charlie like to keep up with the news."

"How is he?"

"Last year, after he give up his saloon and stop going to Warrens, he eat a little more, and drink a little less. For a while, I think he get better. But this year is almost over and he not come downstairs one time. And this month he not get out of bed at all."

"Well, remember, anytime you need help, you give us a ring. That's what the telephone's for."

She glanced up at the thin black wire suspended between the two ranches, thinking of how she had joked when Shepp had suggested it four years ago, how grateful she was for it now.

"You and Shepp already do too much," she said. "You order my seeds, my spectacles, my shoes." Laughing, she pointed to the stream of clear water now officially designated on maps as Polly Creek. "You even order survey men to make me a famous person!"

Pete nodded at the tin loaded with Polly's gifts. "Small payment for this, all the surprise fish fries, and good suppers," he said.

"You come over after you get back from the Jumbo, I make you a chestnut pie and good venison jerky to take with you when you go set your trap line."

Pete patted his stomach. "Don't worry, I will."

Back inside, Polly chopped some leftover chicken for Teddy who had grown toothless, then took down a clean jar to make gum arabic water to soothe Charlie's cough. She poured water, sugar candy, and gum into the jar, set it in a saucepan of water, and stirred.

As she waited for the gum and candy to dissolve, she thought of all the remedies, Chinese and Western, which had failed to cure Charlie's cough or restore his strength. Not for the first time, she wondered if the cough was perhaps a symptom of a more serious illness and not the illness itself. If only Li Dick had not left Warrens, she could ask him, but he had gone back to China and A Can, the retired packer who had taken his place as herbalist for the dozen or so remaining Chinese, did not have Li Dick's skills. Nevertheless, she tried the powders and herbs he ordered for her from the Big City, just as she tried the medicines friends and strangers suggested, the receipts for cures Charlie found in his books.

Steam rose fragrant from the saucepan and she poured the mixture into a mug to take up to Charlie. At the bottom of the stairs, Teddy raised his forepaws expectantly. He was too old, too stiff to climb more than one or two steps, and he pawed at the treads, whining, begging Polly to carry him up too.

Careful not to spill the gum arabic water, she leaned over cautiously and scratched behind his ears, his chin, ruffling his fur. "I come back for you," she promised.

Charlie was asleep. Polly set the steaming mug down on the table beside him and laid the back of her hand against his forehead, his sunken cheek. How thin he had grown, his flesh melting despite custards and rich broths, leaving mere skin over bone. And his cheek, falsely rosy, burned to the touch.

His eyes opened, brightened at the sight of Polly beside him. He pulled her down onto the bed and pointed to the photograph album propped open on his chest. "Look," he said hoarsely.

It was her wedding picture. She stood, stiffly corseted, dress dark and sober, face serious, sad almost, right hand resting awkwardly on Charlie's thick family bible. But underneath, where no one except Charlie and herself would see, she had been afire in scarlet. From her long crimson petticoats to her embroidered corset cover and ruffled drawers.

Polly smiled, remembering. "I dare not wear red outside or everyone think I am shameful, but in China, red is a happy color, a wedding color, so I want to wear it. That's why I look so serious. I'm trying not to laugh and give away our secret."

"It's been twenty-seven years," Charlie said. "Fifty if we go back to the day you first rode into Warrens, trying to act brave when any fool could see how scared you were." A spasm of coughing shook him.

Polly propped him up on his pillows and rubbed

his back. She passed him a square of clean sacking. He spat into it. Phlegm threaded with red wisps. Blood.

She felt the moment freeze. Blood meant the spitting blood disease. The same spitting blood disease she had seen kill men much younger than Charlie.

Blinking back tears, she snatched the soiled piece of sacking and threw it into the can already spilling over with phlegm-stiffened squares of cloth, some traced with the telltale brown of dried blood.

"If only life could be held captive like memories," Charlie sighed.

Unable to speak, Polly closed Charlie's wasted fingers around the mug of gum arabic water and walked over to the window opposite the bed. She rested her forehead against the chilled panes of glass.

Outside, dusk gathered into darkness. Soft and gentle, it rolled down the canyon walls, obliterating the mahogany and scrub oaks flamed red between blue green spruces and lemon yellow aspens and willows. It marched on, relentless, devouring her garden, the vine-covered hen house, the porch, until there was only blackness. A bit of gold flashed, Amber hurrying home? But Amber, shot by a faceless stranger, was dead. Like Bertha Long's second son, a soldier in France, and her husband, John, snatched by death at the end of a dance.

The bit of gold flickered, leaped into a tongue of

fire, and she saw the room and Charlie, ghostly white, reflected in searing flame. A dog howled.

"No," Polly cried, spinning around.

She realized immediately the flame was only Charlie lighting the lamp, the howl Teddy reminding her of her promise. But when she took the empty mug from Charlie, it shattered in her grasp.

A shard pierced her palm. Instinctively she brought it to her lips and sucked the wound. The blood tasted of salt. Like tears.

THIRTY-ONE

During the long winter months, the red stains in Charlie's phlegm had grown larger and darker, his cough more deep seated. But with the coming of the dry summer heat, his cough had eased up, and though he was still too weak to walk, Polly was confident he was on the mend.

She set his empty dinner dishes on the tray. "You know, Bruce Crofoot at Sheep Creek have the spitting blood sickness like you and he come to Salmon River to die. Now he is more healthy than me. You know why? Because he eat mold. All the mold he can find. Especially bread mold."

Charlie dealt out a game of solitaire on the light summer quilt Polly insisted he needed. "Don't get any ideas about feeding me mold," he said.

"What do you think stop your infection when Cox shoot you?" she said, retrieving Teddy's empty bowl from where he lay at the foot of the bed.

"That wasn't any old mold. It was Li Dick's. And I didn't have to eat it."

She peered over Charlie's shoulder. "Put the three of spades there and that queen here," she advised, pointing.

"I thought you were going fishing," he said.

Laughing, she picked up the tray. Teddy pawed at the edge of the bed, silently begging to be carried down and taken with her. She rubbed his nose. "No, Teddy. You stay with Charlie," she said, scratching his chin, his twitching whiskers. "You too old to climb over rocks."

She was getting too old for climbing over blisteringly hot rocks herself, Polly realized, puffing, her heat-swollen feet chaffing against the stiff leather of her brogues. But by August, Polly Creek was too low for good fishing and, with Pete in Dixie, she did not want to disturb Shepp for something so trivial as rowing her over to Crooked Creek.

Scrambling over one final boulder, she set down her rod and tackle, wiped her face free of perspiration, took a few minutes to catch her breath, then unlaced her brogues, pulled off her stockings, and soaked her burning feet in the ice cold water of the Salmon.

The swift current swirled around her feet, soothing, and she closed her eyes and settled back against the smooth hollow of a sun-baked rock. The lacy fronds of willow shading her from the sun created a cool blue green world, and inside Polly, peace and contentment brimmed replete.

When Polly woke, the air had become heavy and threatening, and the sun had already begun its descent in the arc of sky above the canyon rim. She dried her feet quickly on her apron, pulled on stockings and shoes, attached bait to hook, lifted her rod, and cast out. The line curved, sure and graceful, into the gittering white water of the Salmon.

The glare of sun on water hurt her eyes, and she looked beyond the silver streak of river to the sparsely wooded slope rising from the stretch of rocks and sand. In the open space around a deer lick, three or four doe and a young buck became suddenly still, then darted from the hollow. Their big ears and long slim necks flashed between rocky outcrops as they disappeared into tall grasses and pines, leaving Polly jumpy, her senses fractured, yet keenly aware.

She felt the stifling heat that bounced off the canyon walls, heard the nervous chatter of squirrels. Bird cries. Flapping wings. Crackling. The acrid smell of smoke. Her eyes scanned the tree- and brush-covered slopes ahead of her. All clear. She turned. There, rising from behind the thick copse of trees screening the house was the smoke, a thin, innocent spiral. A cooking fire started by a prospector or friend? Then why the flight of deer and squirrels and birds?

The rod slid from Polly's fingers and she
scrambled back over the rocks, heedless of the
sharp edges that snagged her stockings and scraped
her hands.

Her legs, hampered by skirts and fear, grew
heavy. Her rock-torn palms stung. Throat and
lungs burned. Heart pounded, threatening to burst
through chest. But now she could hear Teddy's
mournful wailing, the pounding of hooves against
stable doors, frightened neighing, Charlie's hoarse
cries, and she dared not stop.

At last she was past the rocks and blind of trees
and on the grassy slope to garden and house. A
small tongue of flame licked the peak of the roof
nearest the chimney. A roof fire? And the cedar
shakes drier than the kindling she used to light the
stove. How bad was it? How fast was it spreading? What was happening on the side she could not
see?

Her thoughts raced past her feet. The pole
ladder. The one in the shed. Water. Too far to the
creek. Use the water in the barrel first. Then the
creek. Can't do it alone. Shepp. Telephone him
first. Then the ladder, then the buckets.

Cut across the vegetable patch. Shorter.
Can't. The deer fence. She tore at the poles. Too
deeply embedded. The gate too far. Squeeze
through. Not enough space.

Splinters pierced her skirts, her flesh.

"Polly!"

She whipped around. Shepp was in his rowboat, already halfway across the Salmon. He knew. He was coming. Help was coming!

Hope surged through Polly, giving her the strength to burst through the fence. Her feet crushed cabbages, squashes, melons. She pushed through rows of corn. And then the earth exploded, throwing Polly to the ground. A rifle cracked. And then another, and another, the sharp reports of pistol and rifle ammunition exploding one shell at a time. Dirt filled Polly's mouth, her nose, her ears, her eyes. Fragments of vegetables. Grit. Screams. Drumming hooves. Teddy's barks. The frantic squawking of chickens.

Dazed by her fall, choking from the dust and smoke, Polly pulled herself to her knees. The cabin was completely enveloped in flames.

"Charlie!" she screamed, scrambling to her feet. "Charlie."

With a fierce energy she thought lost forever, Polly broke through the fence, rushed across the strip of yard and tore up the stairs, heedless of the flames that leaped around her.

The smoke upstairs was far thicker and blacker. She covered her nose and mouth with her apron, dropped to her knees, and crawled to their bedroom. Her eyes, unprotected, smarted and teared. Groping, she found the bed. Empty.

"Charlie," Polly called through her apron. "Where are you?"

Smoke burned her throat raw. She coughed. Above the crackle of flames she heard Teddy whimper, felt his tongue wet against her arm. She hugged the dog to her.

"Where's Charlie?" she asked.

Teddy tugged at her sleeve. She crawled behind him. Around the bed. Past the dresser. To the desk beside the washstand. He stopped and pulled feebly at a crumpled quilt beside the open trunk.

Polly fell on the lifeless form beneath it. "Charlie!" she cried.

He stirred, struggling to reach the desk. "Papers. Must get papers," he whispered.

"We have to go," she said, tearing a towel from the rack above the washstand and dunking it into the pitcher of water. "Get out. Now." She wrung out the towel. "You hold towel over your mouth with one hand. Wrap your other arm around me, and..."

Charlie pushed the towel away. "No. Got to get certificates. Claim."

Polly staggered to her feet. "Charlie, please. Help me," she pleaded, trying to pull him upright.

Glowing cinders and ash showered down, sparking small flickering fires. Teddy frisked like a puppy, yelping in pain. Polly, choking from the smoke, the smell of singed fur, and burning flesh, released Charlie to stamp and beat out the flames on the floor, Charlie, Teddy, herself.

"Polly? Charlie?"

"Shepp," Polly called. "Over here." She patted Teddy. "Fetch Shepp," she commanded.

She tore a second towel off the rack and dunked it in the pitcher.

"Here," she said, handing the towel to Shepp. "You take."

Shepp draped the wet towel over his head and shoulders. "Hurry," he said, hoisting Charlie to his feet. "The staircase will go any minute."

Charlie struggled. "No," he coughed. "Papers. Must get papers."

Polly jerked open the drawer of the desk, grabbed a sheaf of papers and waved them in front of Charlie. "I have papers," she said, stuffing them into the bib of her apron.

Quickly, she covered his face with the wet towel and lifted the hem of her apron, making a sling for Teddy.

"Charlie's passed out," Shepp said. "He's dead weight."

"I help," Polly said. Cradling Teddy with one hand, she tried to lift Charlie's legs with the other. She could not.

"Drop the dog," Shepp said.

"No." She stuffed the bunched up apron into her mouth and held it with her teeth, leaving her arms free to lift Charlie's legs.

She backed toward the door. The heat in the hallway was intense. Polly twisted her head to see behind her, but the smoke and flames had created an impenetrable black and orange wall.

"Left," Shepp shouted above the roar of flames and falling timber. "Right. First stair."

Hardly able to breathe, her jaw straining from Teddy's weight, her arms from Charlie's, Polly felt warily for the edge of the stair, lowered one foot, then the next. And again for the second stair. The third.

The awkward angle pushed Charlie's feet against Teddy, tearing at the taut stretch of apron. Polly clenched her teeth tighter. She thrust Charlie's legs stiffly forward from Teddy's bulk, dropped onto another stair, snapped her head back, pulled Charlie's feet back against her belly, and lowered Teddy onto Charlie's legs. Immediately, the pressure on her teeth, jaw, and neck lifted.

She continued the torturous descent. Right foot feel, drop. Left foot follow. Right foot feel, drop. Left foot follow.

Her skin blistered from the profusion of falling cinders. Her eyes teared. She gagged from the choking black smoke, the apron stuffed into her mouth. The weight on her arms, her jaws, and neck became unbearable. She tried pushing Charlie's legs onto one side of her so she could wrap her arms around them more fully, but the movement threatened Teddy's precarious balance in the slackened folds of her apron. Almost there, she told herself, tightening her grip. Right foot feel, drop. Left foot follow. Right foot feel, drop.

Her foot plunged through the stair. Jagged, splintered wood tore through her stockings. Flames seared her scratched flesh. She hurled herself forward, reaching for the banister, pulling her leg back through the charred stair. Teddy squirmed, yelping, burrowing. There was a sudden release of pressure on her teeth and jaws, an emptiness, a long mournful howl. The crash of a falling beam. A shower of cinders. The awful stink of scorched fur and flesh.

"You all right?" Shepp shouted.

Tearing the now useless apron sling from between clenched teeth, Polly coughed a faint, "Yes."

Grimly, she hoisted Charlie's legs back up, clutched the bannister, and half slid, half fell to the bottom of the stairs, staggering around fallen timbers, raging flames, outside to air. Life. And a rain of ashes cold as her own heart.

THIRTY-TWO

From the spare bedroom of Shepp and Pete's house, Polly could not see what was left of Polly Place. Yet there had not been a moment, day or night, in the seven weeks since the fire when the events of that afternoon did not replay themselves in her mind's eye.

Exhausted, choking from smoke and fear, their clothes scorched, and their singed hair and blistered flesh stinking, she and Shepp had carried Charlie to safety, released the horses and cow, and run back and forth from the creek, pouring bucket after bucket of water, stamping and beating out new bursts of flames. The fire had not spread beyond the sheds. But the house was a black skeleton above dead embers, Teddy and twenty-eight years of her life buried in its ashes. And Charlie?

In the gloomy yellow puddle of light cast by the lamp, his bearded face peered corpselike above the bright patchwork of borrowed quilts, radiating questions which haunted like spectres.

What if she had not gone fishing that afternoon? What if she had not fallen asleep down by
the river? What if Charlie had not been so worried
about the papers needed for her protection? Would
he have tried sliding down the stairs on his own
before the explosion, escaping the clouds of black
smoke that had filled his weakened lungs? Or what
if she had not tried to save Teddy, a toothless dog
already close to death? Would Charlie then be free
of this terrible gurgling that sounded increasingly
like a death rattle?

Only an hour ago, when his coughing had
become so severe that breathing became impossible, she had thrust her fingers down his throat,
allowing the phlegm, blood, and corruption to spill
out in curdled lumps, clearing the clogged passages. But already they had refilled, and again his
chest was heaving, his lungs straining for the small
bits of rank sickroom air that grated through the
blocked passages of his nose and throat.

Polly fumbled for the bottle of oil among the jars
and bottles that crowded the nightstand. When she
had inserted her fingers in Charlie's mouth before,
his teeth had clamped down involuntarily, and she
had had to pry open his jaws with her other hand in
order to force her fingers into his throat. She knew
he would not let her try again, yet it was the
constant struggle for air that used up his strength.

She rubbed the oil into the blue gray ridges and
fissures of Charlie's swollen fever-cracked lips,

remembering their smooth, gentle warmth, their ability to please, love, and hurt.

His eyelids fluttered open. He lifted his arm and reached for hers. "The laws haven't changed," he whispered, just as he did each time he woke.

She took his hand, the flesh so shriveled, so cold she could almost feel the pull of death. "I know, but you not worry. I have papers. See?"

She picked up the wedding certificate, certificate of residence, and claim for the ranch, and held them close. He strained forward. The gurgling deep in his chest intensified, and he fell back against the pillows, gasping for air. Polly dropped the papers and added another pillow to the already large pile beneath his head.

"It's no good," he panted. "I'm drowning. Drowning in my own juices."

He coughed. Polly pulled a wad of clean sacking from her apron pocket. She wiped the blood from Charlie's mouth and beard, the perspiration from his forehead, neck, and chest, grieving for his loss of strength, his regression to the helplessness of a child, a baby.

A baby. Hadn't she once saved a baby by taking a reed, pulling out the pithy center to make a hollow tube, working the reed down the baby's throat, and sucking out the mucus? Then why not Charlie? She threw down the soiled sacking. "Charlie, I go get a reed to make tube that can help you breathe."

THIRTY-TWO

He clutched her sleeve, his eyes dark pits of fear. "No. Stay."

"I won't be long. Just a few minutes."

"Pol, you can't save me," he rasped, the rattle from his chest and throat muffling his words so she could scarcely hear him.

Her eyes glistened. "You say that when Cox shoot you. I pull you through then. I can get you through this." Out of the corner of her eye, a tear trickled.

Charlie's fingers touched the tear, traced its passage down her wrinkled cheek. "Let me go."

Unable to speak, Polly stroked his sunken cheeks, his wisps of white hair, and beard.

"Remember how you held me all through the night after Cox shot me?"

She nodded.

"Hold me now."

She climbed onto the bed beside him.

"Hold me tight. Like you did then."

Polly wrapped her arms around Charlie, cradling him, making his strangled fight for breath become her own. For a long time, her chest strained, struggling. Then their breathing became one, and together they sank into a soft, feathery darkness.

When Polly wakened, the moon had risen, filling

the room with its cold white light, turning the rock
face of the canyon a gravestone white. From far
away, she heard a loon cry, the sound a lonely haunt
against the rushing roar of the Salmon. Closer, she
heard the half-audible call of cow to calf, the sharp,
harsh quack of a duck. A dog growled.

She shuddered. Nightsounds, she told herself.
Ordinary nightsounds. And then she understood.
It was not the animal cries that made her shudder,
but the silence. The absolute quiet that had come
while she slept.

She tightened her arms around Charlie, comforted by the real presence of his weight. Then,
resting her face against his, she began to speak,
filling the silence with words.

"Once, a long time ago, a goddess give a man a
pill. She tell him if he eat the pill, he can live
forever. But first he must build up body strength.
So he hide the pill in a ceiling beam and wait.

"One day, his wife see the pill shining in the
moonlight like a pearl. She not know what it is and
she curious, so she put it in her mouth. A noise
frighten her, and she swallow the pill. Straight-
away, she fly out of the window to the moon.

"There, she lonely for her husband, and he
lonely for her. So the goddess give him a charm
which let him visit his wife on the fifteenth day of
each month."

She paused and stared up at the moon, a perfect
white circle of light against the pitch black of the

night sky. "That is why one time each month the moon is especially big and bright.

"Like tonight," she whispered. "Like tonight."

THIRTY-THREE

The chicken, onion, garlic, and parsley Polly needed for croquettes had been diced sufficently fine long ago, but she did not stop chopping, for as long as she kept knife striking meat, vegetables, and board, she could not hear the sounds of death. The whine of Shepp's saw. The pounding of his hammer as he constructed Charlie's coffin. The clang and ring of shovels as Pete, Shultz, and Holmes dug Charlie's grave.

The door to the kitchen swung open, and frosty, late October cold sliced through the warm, nutty smells of corn bread and baking pie. Shepp strode in, a long, narrow plank beneath his left arm. Shultz and Holmes shuffled in behind him, a raw pine coffin awkward between them. Pete shut the door.

They paused a moment, and through the beating of her knife, Polly heard Shultz and Holmes murmur condolences. She wanted to thank them, to tell them she appreciated their coming down from War

Eagle to help, but the lump in her throat refused speech. Instead she merely nodded and increased the frenzied rhythm of knife against board.

The men climbed the stairs. The clump of their boots and the sharp slap of board and coffin against stair treads and walls reverberated through the kitchen. Above, the floorboards creaked, then were silent. The men had reached the bed. The bed where Charlie lay cold and dead. Straining, Polly heard muffled directions. A sudden, concerted heaving. The dull thud of human flesh against wood. Hammer blows.

Stop, she wanted to call. Charlie can't breathe. He won't be able to breathe. But that was foolish. As foolish as thinking she could block out the reality of Charlie's death by pulverizing chicken into inedible mush.

With a single sweep of her knife, Polly scooped the meat and vegetables into a bowl, added a buttery flour paste, seasonings, lemon, a dash of wine. Her hands moved mechanically, molding the mixture into large balls, rolling the balls in cracker crumbs, dropping them into boiling lard. The grease sizzled, splattered against her hands, stinging. But she felt only the painful scraping and bumping of coffin against stairwell walls, the sudden pause at the turn, suppressed curses.

And then the men were in the kitchen beside her, their breathing heavy, like Charlie's. No, not Charlie. Never again Charlie.

Polly set the croquettes in the warming oven and pulled on coat, gloves, hat. She opened the door and followed the men and Charlie out across the yard, around the house, and behind the root cellar to the grave, an open wound in the hard earth beneath the pines.

Feeling as dry and brittle as the dead leaves scattered in the dirt, she stood at the foot of the grave, longing for the comforting fragrance of incense to smother the smell of raw pine and freshly dug earth. The shrieks and wails of mourners so she would not hear the slither of coffin grazing rope, the sudden banging of wood against rocky outcrops, the soft roll and thud of Charlie within.

Pete cleared his throat. "The Lord giveth, the Lord taketh away, blessed be the name of the Lord."

He hurled a thick clod of soil into the narrow rectangular hole. "From earth to earth, dust to dust, ashes to ashes." He crossed himself.

The men reached for their shovels. Rock and dirt fell on wood, the sound heavy, final. A mist of dust rose around Polly, thickening, like the haze of fine soot that had coated her as she sifted through the charred remnants of her life with Charlie.

There was the elk antler which had hung over the door of Charlie's saloon. The range with the high warming oven and reservoir which she had bought when she first started her boarding house. The bed she and Charlie had shared for almost fifty years. The bowl that had been Teddy's. Charlie's fiddle. The coffee pot kept ready for passing prospectors, friends. All burned, melted, and twisted into shapeless, broken bits of rubbish which crumbled beneath her shovel like so much dust.

Suddenly, through the mist of dust and years, she saw her father crumbling the brick from the kang, mixing it with sooty scrapings, ashes, ground bone, and gristle, shoveling the lot into the narrow hole that had been their fertilizer pit.

She darted to the edge of the half-filled grave. "Stop."

Taken by surprise, all four men stopped their shoveling.

"What is it?" Shepp asked.

Polly thrust her gloved hands into her pockets to hide their trembling. "You tired. Walk all the way to War Eagle for Shultz and Holmes," she told him.

"I'm fine."

"Shultz and Holmes have a long way back."

"It's all right. We're almost done," Holmes said.

"You're hungry, must eat first. Go eat the dinner I make."

"She's right," Pete agreed. "You three go ahead. I'll finish."

Polly seized his shovel. "No, I finish."

"You can't do it alone," Pete protested.

"I plow. I dig the garden. I can bury my man."

Shultz and Holmes looked from Shepp to Pete, questioning.

"Please, I want to be alone."

The men left reluctantly. She waited until they filed past the corner of the root cellar and out of sight. Then, leaning her whole weight against the shovel she held, she gave in to exhaustion and grief.

Late afternoon shadows stained the pines ink green. The canyon walls, imprisoning as the walls of Charlie's grave, closed in on Polly, suffocating, refusing comfort, their dark pockets somber echoes of the frozen emptiness that held her fast.

She heard footsteps crunch against gravel, shovels scraping into earth, realized Shepp and Pete had come to finish filling Charlie's grave. She wanted to help. To make Charlie safe from scavenging coyotes. But she was too tired. And so she remained standing, stock still, like the long-legged wading birds with webbed feet and slender bills that she and Charlie watched in winter.

Sometimes singly, sometimes in pairs, they stood absolutely motionless on the rocks at the edge of the Salmon, waiting to regain their strength. She had seen a full day pass, even two, before a bird took wing again. But always, no matter how tired and faltering their first nervous flutters, the birds pressed inexorably back into flight.

Clumsily, she pressed cold, cramped muscles into motion, and above the noise of scraping shovels

and falling earth, she said, "Tomorrow I go
Warrens."

PART SIX

第六部份

1922-1923

THIRTY-FOUR

The children, their coats, hats, scarves, and stockings streaks of color against the mourning white of winter, ripped through the gash in the timber on their homemade skis, some tumbling, others expert, their laughter shrill, their wind-whipped faces flushed with fierce, energetic delight. A bundle of fur, wool, and two long, slender pieces of planed wood rolled into the soft drift of snow near Polly. She heard muffled sobs.

"You okay?" Polly called.

The shapeless bundle shaking off loose snow laughed. "Sure."

"Who cry?" Polly asked, puzzled.

The bundle cocked her head. "Sound's coming from the back of the school house so it's probably Gay Carrey. She's always hiding behind the wood pile to cry."

Her walk rolling and awkward, Polly stumbled across the gray brown snow trampled hard by dozens of booted feet to the narrow path cleared between the school house and the woodpile stacked high as the roof. In the shadows, a girl, no more than five or six, crouched on a fallen log, tears streaming down chapped cheeks.

Above her, a boy only a few years older, hovered, pleading. "It's no use crying. You know you can't go home."

Polly rummaged in her coat pocket. Out came handkerchief, fish hook, candies. "You the Carrey children from South Fork?"

The boy, eyeing the candies in Polly's gloved hand, nodded.

His cheeks, red and bulging as though he had swallowed two apples, and his big eyes, transparent with desire, made Polly smile. "Then you are Johnny," she said, extending her hand.

He took a candy. "Thanks. Who're you?"

His question, innocent and ordinary, hurt Polly deeper than she would have guessed possible. There was a time when there would have been no need for questions, when every child knew her just as she had known them, their birthdays, their likes and dislikes. But after almost thirty years absence, only a few were faintly recognizable as children of the children she had nursed and loved. More were as unfamiliar as Warrens itself, with the hundreds of Chinese who had placered Warrens Meadow gone, the meadow carved into craters by steam-powered shovels, and the buildings in the camp all new since the fire in 1903.

She popped a candy into Gay's mouth. Too startled to object, the child sucked noisily, her sobs diminishing. Polly squatted on the log beside her. She wiped Gay's eyes and nose, straightened the knitted stocking cap.

"My name is Polly," she told Johnny. "One time five years ago, you play the fiddle with my husband, Charlie Bemis, in his dance hall. I not there, but he tell me about it. He say you play real good."

Anxious to waylay questions about Charlie, she rushed on. "This your first winter in school?"

"Not mine, Gay's. She's homesick."

Fresh tears spilled down Gay's cheeks. She smeared them with the back of her mittened hands. "I am not, I just hate her!" she declared vehemently.

"Who?"

The boy pointed to the teacher who had come out to the yard. Tall, rawboned, and sternly gaunt, she rang the bell, signaling the end of noon recess. "I board with Francis's mother, Mrs. Rodin, the lady that runs the big hotel," Johnny explained. "But Gay boards with the teacher. She's horrible. Can't boil water and says we get on her nerves. Poor Gay has to sleep in her bed, and she has garlic breath and snores and takes up all the room!"

The yard filled with chatter, laughter, the clatter of skis, the stamping and scraping of boots. As the teacher shouted at the stragglers, Polly felt the child tremble beside her, saw the lips quiver, threatening the fragile dam of tears.

She pinched the child's cheek tenderly. "The teacher frighten you?"

Johnny took Gay's mittened hands and pulled. "Come on, we'd better go or there'll be trouble."

Gay slid off the log reluctantly. Eyes riveted on Polly, she trailed behind her brother, her little legs in their high buckled overshoes making two steps for his every one. Polly started after them. But before she reached the schoolhouse door, the teacher slammed it.

Walking back to the one-room cabin Pete had rented for her, Polly wondered if her own loneliness for Charlie and their life together in the canyon was clouding her judgment, making her see an urgency in the child that did not exist.

Ever since the school in Warrens had been built, families in outlying ranches who wanted educations for their children had boarded them out for the school year. The separations were hard on parents and children, but unavoidable, and Gay, like her brother, would adjust if only she did not have to live with that grim-faced tartar.

The thought brought Polly to a halt. Why did Gay have to stay with the teacher when she could come live with her? Of course, they would have to share the one bed in the cabin, but she was much smaller than the teacher. And, Polly chuckled softly, she was sure she didn't have garlic breath. Or snore.

Gay's tears vanished once she moved in with Polly. At noon recess and after school, she and Johnny joined the other children skiing down the mountain slope, playing dare base and pullaway, and in the late afternoons and early evenings before Johnny went back to Mrs. Rodin's hotel and Gay slept, Polly's cabin filled with laughter, the warm buttery fragrance of popping corn, the sweet stickiness of taffy pulls.

With the children, Polly found even the most ordinary tasks took on new color and life. They dyed eggs with onion and walnut shells and cut cookies in the shapes of animals and clouds. While Polly dressed a hen for supper, Johnny blew up the cleaned-out chicken crop, tossing it like a balloon. And when Polly made bread, Gay, her face and long-sleeved gingham apron streaked with flour, stood on a chair, neighing, while her hands, pretend horses, plunged into dough, then pawed their way back up the steep sides of the bowl and down again.

Often, Johnny would make the mile walk to Slaughter Creek to borrow a fiddle from the Adams children. Then, face fixed in serious concentration, he would tuck the fiddle under his chin and, as bow flew across fiddle turning out merry tunes, Polly would find herself back in time with Charlie.

The days, golden as sunbeams, slid into weeks and months, and winter gave way to spring. Long underwear, leggings, thick-ribbed stockings, flannel petticoats and heavy wool dresses peeled off layer by layer, and they gave up indoor baking, story telling, singing, and stereoscope views for kite flying, fishing, and picnics. Soon, spotted trout, too tiny to eat, swam in jars on window ledges spilling over with cans of sprouting seeds and bouquets of wild flowers gathered on long rambles. And soon, all too soon, school would be over, and Gay and Johnny going home.

Polly's fingers lightly brushed the child sleeping beside her. If her days and nights after Charlie's death had been long and dark before Gay came to brighten them, how would she bear them when Gay left?

Abruptly, she rose and padded across the cabin to the stove, opened the damper and draft, and shook the grate. The coals flashed sparks which, shiny as false gold, crumbled into ash. Like her few fleeting months with the child, Polly thought as she built a new fire.

For a long time, she stood, staring into the bright new flames, holding her hands out to them, warming. Then she turned, lit the lamp, and carried it over to the dresser. The old Bull Durham tin she took from beneath the fabric scraps in the bottom drawer was cold to the touch. She held it lightly, reluctant to open it, knowing she must. Finally, she pried it open.

The lingering, bittersweet fragrance of Charlie's favorite tobacco assailed Polly's nostrils. She inhaled hungrily, but the scent was too thin and too soon gone to satisfy. Feeling cheated, she took out the papers she had stuffed inside after Charlie died. Brittle with age and too much folding, they crackled as she spread them out. Her wedding certificate. Her certificate of residence. The mining claim for the ranch. The papers for which Charlie had been willing to give up his life. The papers she would gladly surrender to bring him back.

Unwanted tears blurred the papers, the child on the bed. Polly rubbed her eyes, impatient. After Gay went home, she would go to Grangeville to visit Bertha and get fitted for new spectacles.

THIRTY-FIVE

In the far corner of Bertha Long's kitchen, Polly, the parrot, strutted across its cage, jumped onto its perch, ruffled its brilliant green and gold feathers, and pecked at its empty dish, demanding, "Polly wants breakfast. What does Polly want for breakfast? Polly wants something for breakfast!"

Polly, slicing cherries at the work table between the stove and sink, shook her knife at the bird. "Polly be quiet or Polly be breakfast!" she warned.

Bertha laughed. "Do you remember when Brown complained about your coffee and you jumped out from behind the stove, waving your cleaver, and shouting, 'Who not like my coffee?'"

Chuckling, Polly stirred the chopped cherries into the bowl of cookie batter. "Brown tell me my coffee is too strong. Your husband say it's too weak. After I shake my knife, they both say my coffee is the best!"

"Having you here is like having the old times back," Bertha said, still laughing. She pulled a handkerchief from her pocket and dried her eyes. "I can almost believe my John and your Charlie aren't dead, and that I'm not a fat old woman with stiff rheumatic knees."

"I'm glad I come. Grangeville have so many old friends and at the same time so many new things I never see or try before."

"What have you enjoyed the best?"

"Let's see," Polly said, dropping teaspoons of batter onto a cookie tray.

There was the excitement of her ride in the stage, one of the new wagons that needed neither horse nor mule to pull. The warm welcome of old friends. The unexpected kindness and curiosity of strangers like Mr. Shaffley, the editor from the Idaho Free Press who had come to interview her at Jennie Holmes' house; the school teacher who had brought his daughter to see her; the little girl, Verna, who had walked all the way across town just to take her photograph and ask a few questions. And of course, there were the fine shops where generous friends reawakened her vanity by buying her new clothes. The new gold-rimmed spectacles that made the hills and wheat fields look freshly washed and her friends and herself twice as old. The trips to the nickleodeon and, even better, the moving pictures.

"Mary Pickford," she decided, scraping the last of the batter from around the bowl. "We go see 'The Love Light' again, okay?"

"I thought you found 'The Love Light' embarrassing," Bertha teased.

"Never mind, I cover my face with my hands and only look through my fingers."

Bertha, shaking seed into the bird dish, began to laugh, scattering the seed over the linoleum floor. The bird flapped its wings furiously. "Polly's breakfast," it squawked. "Where's Polly's breakfast?"

Polly swept the seed up and poured it into the bird's dish. "There, you silly old bird."

"You mean you'd rather see 'The Love Light' than go on a train ride?" Bertha said.

Polly's eyes widened. "Train? Here? Charlie say we never see the railroad."

"Not in the Salmon Canyon maybe, but we've had the railroad here for years."

Polly whipped off her apron. "Then what we wait for? Let's go."

When the trainmen heard that Polly had never seen a locomotive or cars before, they lifted her into the engine cab and opened the firebox. The blast of hot air sprayed soot all over her starched white dress, but she was too excited to care. As long as she had been in America, she had heard of the iron road. Charlie had told her that there were tracks laid all across the continent, and she knew many of the Chinese in Warrens had helped build it. Now that she was finally going to ride in one, she wanted to see everything. The great solitary reflecting lamps in front above the cow guards, the seething, roaring furnace that fed the engines, the baggage cars loaded with produce and grain, the smoking cars, sleeping cars, even the tiny, cramped lavatories.

A bell tolled. With a shriek of the train whistle, the metal wheels ground against the tracks, and she and Bertha were flung against the prickly green plush seats. Trees, mountains, wheat fields, horses, and wagons flew past in a blur.

"Now you've done everything," Bertha shouted above the rhythmic clickety-clack of wheels.

"Oh no," Polly shouted back. "I only just begin. After I go back to Warrens, my old boarder, Jay Czizek, and his wife take me to Boise."

Boise was a spectacular city of tall buildings with moving boxes which took the place of stairs, street cars, gas and electric lights, and a huge park complete with joy wheel, fun factory, miniature railroad, ostrich farm, picture show building, and a natatorium where men and women, practically naked, swam in a huge, steamy enclosed pool. But, pacing the thick pile carpet of her room at the Idanha Hotel, it was none of these wonders that

Polly thought about. Instead, a conversation she had overheard replayed itself.

She had been on the street car leaving Chinatown after her visit with Bob No. 2 who had worked for Bob Katon in Warrens, and there had been two male Chinese voices, low and intense.

"When I was a young man, there was no food in my village. I had to come to America, but China is different now. Won't you change your mind and come with me?"

"No, Uncle. This is my home."

"I have worked here forty of my sixty years, but I do not call it home."

"I was born here"

"An old man like me goes back to China to die. But you are young. You can help build our country, make it strong."

"My country, my home is here."

"And where is my home?" Polly had whispered. Not in China, a faded memory. Or Warrens. Or Grangeville. Or Boise. Then where?

The question had repeated itself during her tour of the big city stores, the White City park, even during the motion picture with the short, funny-looking tramp called Charlie. His tiny black mustache, bowler hat, and crazy antics had made her laugh. Yet there had been a frantic sadness about him, as though he dared not stop.

Like herself.

The unexpected comparison caught Polly short.

THIRTY-FIVE

She stopped her pacing. The room with its bright fire, heavy drapes, and clutter of furniture closed in on her, and she lifted the window sash and leaned out.

It was late, but the street and buildings were brightly lit, voiding the sky of stars, and though she could see the faint glow of moonlight, the height of the buildings blocked the moon itself.

All at once, a wave of homesickness engulfed Polly, sweeping away doubts and fears in a crest of longing. She knew where she belonged.

THIRTY-SIX

Bird song woke Polly. She had arrived too late the night before to see anything more than deep shadows and starlight, but the warm embrace of the canyon walls and the welcoming roar of the Salmon had told her she was home, and she had fallen asleep dreaming of the rustle of wind through tall, healthy corn stalks, the smell of new cut hay, the taste of bread made from her own wheat, milk warm from her own cow. Now, eager to see the ranch in daylight, she threw off her shawl and stretched.

The seventeen mile walk down the steep trail from Warrens and the night spent on the cold, hard ground of the root cellar had taken a deeper toll than she anticipated, and her muscles, cramped and sore, resisted movement. Unalarmed, in fact rather enjoying the teasing suspense the delay evoked, Polly worked the knots in her arms and legs loose, then rose and pushed open the door.

At first she thought her eyes, dazzled by the

sudden light, deceived her. Then she realized she had merely deceived herself. Polly Place, like Charlie, was gone forever. Angrily, she ripped at the dew wet weeds and brittle grasses around her.

"Polly! What are you doing here?"

She looked up at Pete, startled, forgetting how the night before she had playfully spread her white hankerchief on a bush facing the river to announce she was back.

"I couldn't believe it when I saw your old signal for help, but I thought I'd better check it out. When did you get here? Is something wrong?"

Polly's fingers closed around the black earth beneath the pulled weeds and grasses. She smelled its dampness, felt its heavy richness, the warmth of the sun sweeping down the pine-clad canyon walls, the rushing roar of the Salmon.

"For a long time, yes. But not now, not anymore," she said.

"Polly, you're not making sense."

She smiled. "You see, after Charlie die, I hurt so much, I think I must get away. But I wrong. Charlie's not just here in the canyon. He's inside me, and it does not matter where I go, Warrens, Grangeville, or Boise, he be there. There and not there. That is what hurt. But nothing will change that, and this canyon is my home. Our home. So I come back."

Pete's arms made a wide sweep, taking in the fences torn down by bears, the garden trampled back into the earth, the sagging chicken house overrun with trailers of hops, thirty years' work work reclaimed by the canyon in one. "There's nothing left."

She opened her hand, revealing the rich black soil. "I have the land."

"You know how much work it took to make your ranch," Pete said gently.

"And I'm too old to start over," she said for him.

"Yes."

"I know I never have big ranch like before, and I not need. All I want is a small house and help with heavy work."

She reached into her pocket, pulled out Charlie's old Bull Durham tin, forced open the lid, and took out a piece of paper. "This is Charlie's mining claim for twenty acres. Help me build a house and make a small garden, and when I die, bury me next to Charlie. Then the claim is yours and you can homestead the land."

"You don't have to do that," Pete said gruffly.

Polly smiled. "You think when I die I can take the land with me?" She spread the claim open and held it out to Pete. "You agree?"

For a moment the paper fluttered in the morning breeze. Then Pete reached for it, folded it, and put it in his pocket.

"Welcome home," he said.

PART SEVEN

第七部份

1933

THIRTY-SEVEN

The salmon thrashed, jerking against the line that meant its certain death. At the same time, Polly, wedged firmly behind a rock, whirled the reel, rapidly letting out more slack. Then, at just the right moment, she tightened the line until it became taut. Again the fish fought hard, threatening to snap the slender strand that snared it, and again, Polly's fingers twirled expertly to release the tension. Like a cat with a mouse, she continued to play with the fish until, exhausted, it offered no resistance when she wound in her line.

Laughing at the contrast between the ten-inch squaw fish at the end of her line and the salmon of her daydream, Polly unhooked the fish and threw it in the creel with the five she had caught earlier.

"Never mind," she told the fish. "You small and you bony, but you just right for old lady."

She threw her unused bait into Polly Creek, picked up creel and rod, and started up the grassy slope to the cabin Shepp and Pete had built for her. It was not far, but she climbed slowly, studying the wild sumac, buttercups, towering pines, and firs like a person scrutinizing the face of an old friend, for beneath the blue canopy of sky and within the rock face and timbered slopes were countless memories. Memories she had tried to run from, but which she had learned to treasure, mulling over them, in conversation or alone, just as she and Charlie had once reviewed the photographs in the album the fire had destroyed.

She sank down on the porch steps to catch her breath. Sunshine poured down on her, penetrating the lightly quilted percale dress lined with outing flannel that she had made for summer wear. The rays warmed, easing the rheumatism that had settled in her joints, and once again Polly congratulated herself for choosing a site where the sun, as soon as it rose over the rim of the canyon, would shine through her curtainless loft window, and where, from her porch, she could catch the last rays as it sank out of sight. She closed her eyes, basking like a contented cat until her breath returned. Then she picked up creel and rod and went inside.

Pete said the cabin was not much more than a doll's house, with space downstairs only for the smokey wood stove she kept threatening to replace, and the chairs and table Shepp had made, and upstairs, in the sleeping loft where only she could stand completely straight, a bed and dresser, also made by Shepp. But with the lace-trimmed muslin curtains she had made for the downstairs windows, the rag rug she had hooked, the photograph of Charlie, and bundles of fragrant herbs and spices, it was home, and she had lived in it well content for ten years.

Not waiting for her eyes to adjust to the dim light, she fumbled for the telephone Shepp had installed. Cradling the receiver, she turned the crank and shouted into the speaker.

"Shepp? How many eggs you get today?"

"Six? I get ten," she countered proudly. "How many fish you catch?"

"None? You no good," she chortled. "Never mind, you and Pete come over, I cook squaw fish I catch today, okay?"

"Good. See you later."

She hung the receiver back in place and bustled out to the vegetable patch to pick vegetables to cook with the fish.

With each passing year, her garden had shrunk as her strength had waned. Now she cultivated barely half an acre, and the hen house sheltered only a handful of chickens. But Pete and Shepp brought her wild game and she had more than sufficient food for her needs and those of visitors, old and new. She surveyed the rows of melon, beans, corn, and cabbages drooping in the August heat. Before she picked anything, she would have to water.

Fetching water from the creek had become an increasingly difficult chore, so she watered sparingly, a dipperful at the base of each plant, just as her father had taught her. At the end of each row, she straightened slowly, kneading the small of her back. Halfway through, her head grew swollen and heavy. Black spots danced before her eyes. She pushed on stubbornly. The spots receded, then surged forward, becoming red and gold, then black again.

Then it was all black.

A numbing heaviness sealed Polly's lids so she could not see, but the steady buzzing seemed like the drone from one of the new flying machines that sometimes soared above the canyon. Faint at first, it became louder and louder, rising above the thunder and crash of the Salmon.

She knew she must signal it. She opened her mouth to shout. No sound came. She struggled to rise, but her limbs refused to obey. The droning became faint, then louder, then faint again, until finally it faded, and there was only the familiar roar of the Salmon.

Then there were voices. Shouting. She felt herself gathered up. Bound. Trussed like a chicken for market.

"No, Baba. No," she cried, straining against the

arms that held her. "Some other way, Baba, I beg you. I don't want to go."

His voice, warm and kind, began a comforting murmur, but the grip that held her remained as tight. She knew she was lost, her efforts too feeble against his strength. Still she struggled until, once again, darkness overcame her.

A sudden fierce jolting shot vicious bolts of fire through Polly, shattering the numbing darkness. She mourned it like a lost lover. Why the agonizing punishment when she had given up the struggle long before, she wanted to ask. But her tongue, thick and swollen, prevented her, and she suffered in silence, yearning for the darkness to return and smother her pain.

It came and went, like surf against the shore, sometimes generous, sometimes meager, sometimes simply hovering on the edges of her pain, its promise of relief cruelly tantalizing.

A star glittered silver bright and she searched for moon glow.

"Charlie?" she whispered.

"He's dead, Polly. You know that."

She forced her eyes open. Above her loomed a white man's face, weathered and bearded, no different from the faces of a thousand others, except, on his chest a bit of silver flashed. Silver, sharply edged. A star. The sheriff.

"Paper," she croaked through cracked lips. "I have paper."

THOUSAND PIECES OF GOLD

He seized her arm. Silver glittered, pierced her
skin, bringing peace.

THIRTY-EIGHT

A heavy weight bore down on Polly's chest and limbs, making breathing difficult. Impossible. So this was death, she thought. Confinement in a narrow, airless coffin pressed down by six feet of earth. But if she were dead, then surely she would not be able to feel pain. Doubt bubbled, bursting into panic. It was a mistake. They had thought her dead, buried her too soon. Her arms flailed weakly, ineffectually, against the constricting boundaries.

"Polly! Polly! Can you hear me?"

With a tremendous effort of will, Polly reined in her terror so she could think. She had asked Shepp and Pete to bury her beside Charlie, next to the river they both loved, but the voice calling her was not his. It was a woman's.

"Wake up, Polly. Wake up now," the bodiless voice urged.

Wake up? Then she was not dead, not buried. She struggled to open her eyes. The lids burst open, fluttered against the painful glare of light, and closed again.

"That's it. Come on, you can do it."

Using her lashes to shield her eyes from the hurtful brightness, Polly opened them a little at a time.

Above her, a big strong woman with curly brown hair hovered, encouraging. "That's it. A little more. Come on.

Pale blue walls. White ceiling. Wood stove. Chair. Curtains rippling in a cool breeze. The harsh smells of antiseptics, medicine.

"Hospital?" Polly croaked, her voice as much a stranger's as the woman's.

The woman smiled. "You're in the County Hospital in Grangeville. I'm Eva Weaver, your nurse."

Broken pieces of memory surfaced briefly, blindingly. Men. Horses. Pain. Darkness. A sheriff. Fear. Sirens. Polly struggled to fit the pieces, but reaching for one, she lost another.

"When I come?" she whispered.

The nurse smoothed the sheet that covered Polly, pulling it taut. "You've been here three days. There for a while we thought we would lose you, but you'll be fine now."

Three days! Again, Polly fought to remember. Bits and pieces glimmered, teasing, then vanished, swept away by black waves that, even now, threatened to pull her down.

"I not remember."

"You must have been working in your garden when you took sick," the nurse explained. "Mr. Shepp and Mr. Klinkhammer found you there unconscious. They took you to the War Eagle Mine by horseback though how they got through those steep trails without falling and breaking everyone's neck is anyone's guess. Then the Deputy Sheriff and Nurse brought you here in Glen Ailor's ambulance."

Heat. Thirst. Weariness. Memory or reality? Her head hurt.

"Tired," Polly murmured.

The nurse leaned over Polly, starched uniform crackling. "Of course. You go back to sleep and rest. You have lots of people asking for you. Mr. Klinkhammer, Mr. Shepp, Mrs. Holmes, Mrs. Shultz, Mr. Cyczik, Mrs. Long..."

The names trailed off, disappearing as Polly sank into a deep, restful sleep.

When she woke again, late afternoon sunshine streamed through the open window. While the nurse's daughter held Polly, Mrs. Weaver plumped her pillows, propping her up so she could drink the beef broth they had brought. Polly held the bowl, but feeling no hunger, looked out the window, feasting instead on the cloudless blue sky, the wide expanse of golden prairie rimmed by big buttes, the mountains beyond.

And then she saw them. The gray granite slabs just beyond the picket fence. Headstones. A graveyard. What had Mrs. Weaver said? Struggling, she forced the words to surface. "You're in the County Hospital." The hospital for indigents. Where old men and women went to die.

She thought of her small hoard of nuggets, the gold buttons Charlie had made her, the ones she changed from dress to dress. She dipped the spoon into the soup and drank. She was not indigent. And she was not going to die. Not here.

"Put my shoes next to the bed," she told Mrs. Weaver.

"You're too weak to walk yet."

"Today. But I want shoes there ready for when I can."

The doctor came. Old friends and curious strangers visited, smiling encouragement as the days inched into weeks, the weeks into months. But the shoes beside Polly's bed remained untouched.

"You'll soon get well," Bertha said.

Polly looked at the shoes on the floor, the graveyard outside covered with snow. "I'm too old to get well," she said.

"Don't give up now."

Polly patted her friend's hand. "After Charlie shot, you tell me the same thing. You help me to save his life that time. I know you want to do the same now. But it's not possible. We young then, old now. I have to go to the other world to get well."

Her grip on Bertha tightened. "When I am dead, help me to find Shepp and Pete. Remind them I want bury beside Charlie."

"I will."

EPILOGUE

On November 6, 1933, Polly Bemis died at the Idaho County Hospital in Grangeville. Due to heavy snows, all trails into the Salmon River were impenetrable and neither Charles Shepp nor Pete Klinkhammer could be located. With the City Council of Grangeville acting as pallbearers, Polly was buried in the cemetery she could see from her window.

Her gold nuggets, the gold buttons Charlie had made her, and other effects were donated to St. Gertrude's Museum by Pete Klinkhammer who homesteaded Polly Place.

When he died in 1970, Klinkhammer's sister, heir to his estate, purchased a stone for Polly's grave. The marker reads:

POLLY BEMIS

Sept. 11, 1853 - Nov. 6, 1933

PHOTO CREDITS

Part I — Chinese girl with bound feet. Courtesy of the Bancroft Library.

Part II — Chinese slave girl in a Chinatown bagnio. From *Pigtails and Gold Dust* by Alexander McLeod. Courtesy of the Caxton Printers and the San Francisco History Room, San Francisco Public Library.

Part III — Warrens, Idaho. Courtesy of the Idaho Historical Society.

Part IV — Lalu/Polly Nathoy on her wedding day, August 13, 1894. Courtesy of the Idaho Historical Society.

Part V — Polly Place, the Bemis ranch. Courtesy of John Carrey.

Part VI — Polly Bemis, Grangeville, 1923. From *The River of No Return* by R.G. Bailey. Courtesy of the Idaho Historical Society.

Part VII — Polly Bemis on the porch of her house on the Salmon River. Courtesy of the Idaho Historical Society.

Ruthanne Lum McCunn, a Eurasian of Chinese and Scottish descent, has published seven books on the experiences of Chinese people in America, including the highly acclaimed *Chinese American Portraits: Personal Histories 1828-1988* and her most recent novel, *Wooden Fish Songs*. Her award-winning books have been translated into eight languages. A former teacher, she lives in San Francisco and lectures extensively at schools, universities, and community organizations.